RANTINGS OF A GIRL ON A PATH

By Rachael Hinkley

A true account of a path laid and lost, to be reignited from the ashes the vessel created. An accurate depiction of chaos, love, strength, and becoming, with a little humor for flavor.

"You reach a point on your path where you do not require a single person to understand or relate to you."
                              -Maryam Hasnaa

Copyright 2022 by Rachael Hinkley

All rights reserved. No part of this book may be reproduced, stored in a retrieval system or transmitted in any form, or by any means, without the prior written permission of the author or publisher except by a reviewer who may quote brief passages to be printed in a newspaper, magazine or journal.

First Edition

First Printing

Published by Perfect Trust Productions

www.perfecttrrustproductions.com

1

Ever wonder why we can't remember things before a certain age? Yeah, me too. Sure, there are books and studies and so many different people stating that their explanations are true and accurate. Saying that we can't remember infancy or toddler age is because the mind is too young or that we can, it's just been suppressed by the trauma of birth, memories, and milestones. That very well may be, however, I have a different theory if you will. One that resonates with my soul. I am a believer in past lives, and I believe that for a soul to be born, one must die. The old soul, if you will, is placed in the new soul just before the birth. And I believe the reason a baby cries when the cord is cut is symbolic of the old souls severed ties with their old life. Now stay with me here. I promise this won't be one of THOSE books. I swear I'm going somewhere with this.

I believe that the old soul fights to stay and during infancy up to let's say first words, the old soul is in a constant struggle with letting go and becoming something new. Afraid perhaps to begin a new path, a new life. Not realizing that they wouldn't go anywhere, they would just evolve, change, grow into something they never thought they would or something they wished they had. So, this struggle, this transition if you will, takes place in these years causing a storm in the psyche, one that is conquered by the help of parents and caregivers. Think about this for a moment, did you immediately say 'mama' or 'dada'?? Nope it was a constant reminder of repetitious acts and words from the perspective parent to get you to say those words. When things are done in repetition whether to you or by your own hand, it's an ingrained and instilled thought process right? You learn it, you retain it, it becomes you! It changes you into something different. Sometimes even against your own will, against every fiber of your being. A psychic war being waged between the old soul and the acceptance of it becoming new.

    I have always felt like I didn't belong in the family I was born into. Although my physical characteristics say, *'girl you look just like them!'* my attitude, my thought process, my belief system, says that I am a chess piece in a checker game. I spent the better part of my years trying to figure out why and wasted those years fighting against the path I was meant to be on. To find the path that sets my soul on fire that awakens who I am.

    I knew from a young age I wanted to be somebody; I just didn't know who. I love music, absolutely love it. Something about the cadences awakening every fiber, every nerve. I taught myself to sing, with the help of my grandmother I learned to read music, and I remember thinking, yes this, this is what I want to do. I want to be a professional singer. I would hold concerts in my room for my stuffed animals and baby dolls, Ken was a fan but Barbie not so much. I knew every word to every song of Cindy Lauper's *'Girls just want to have fun'* cassette album, both sides. Yes, for all you youngin's there was a music platform called a cassette tape. It came after the eight track and before the CD, where you had to manually fast-forward, rewind, and flip over when one side was done to listen to the rest of the songs. But I digress.

I literally wore that tape out, I would pause it, rewind and listen to a section over and over until I had it down. When I was in the fourth grade, I saw a school concert that the middle school put on and I said yep, I'm going to do that all the way to college. Yes, I have found my path, my calling, my place at the ripe old age of ten. I mean at 8,9,10 years old we all knew what we wanted, right? Was this really the path I needed to be on? Seemed fitting at the time. We all have these aspirations, these dreams, some of us only dream, others try our hand at achieving them and very few succeed at obtaining them. But who's dreams are they? Yours? Your parents? Or your soul's?

At that time, I could not answer that question. I had a vision of standing in the spotlight and hearing my name echo through an arena. Such a notion to have of a dream so young. But fate had other plans for my ventures, and I would find out that fate was a bitch to be reckoned with. You see little did I know that that dream of singing my heart out, that path that I created, would be ripped up, plowed over, and set ablaze. Why? Because my soul said *'no girl, this is not your path. '*

Oh, I would continue to try, boy did I. I joined the school choir, and I tried my hand at writing music. Turns out you have to have a talent for putting musical notes to words and making them work. Whodathunk? Writing I could do, was quite good at it, but not so much in the musically inclined aspect. Coming from the family that I did, let's just say music lessons were not an option. This would be one of many times I wish I were a boy. Seriously, my brothers got what they wanted. Want to play drums? Bought a drum set and joined the band. Play football? Daddy taught them. Want to draw? Got an easel. I wanted to do things but it wasn't in the budget, or I couldn't because I was a girl. What the hell does that mean? So that path of rockin' out to the best of them fizzled out worse than a one hit wonder.

Paths are not man made, they are, in my opinion, predetermined walkways meant to lead you in the direction of your purpose, of your soul's resting place. I do not mean death here, I mean the place where you can say,*" Ah this is my home, my soul's home, I am finally at peace completely, immensely. I am finally where I belong."* We go through life on paved pathways, constructed by outside sources that try to influence our inner being and manipulate to their will of what and how we are supposed to be. Those outside sources are our environment, our upbringing, ourselves.

I have been known to sabotage my own path that I entirely laid myself. Only to get pissed off that it did not lead me to where I belonged. I have laid many paths for myself, even had a plan written down on paper and was taking steps to execute said plan. To have that very plan halted by circumstances, that a healthy upbringing would have prevented. Teenage pregnancy. Now do not for one second think that I regretted my boy, Nopem he in himself saved me from a fatal path my upbringing set me on, However, had I had the knowledge I do now, then, I would have chosen better, known better, but remember when I said we were all a product of our raising, yep, me too.

The path of motherhood for my mother was not one she should have ventured down, but again, not in control here.

Paths to me are predetermined, predestined, rough, rugged, divinely made, walkways. Designed to direct you to yourself. There are many forks in the path, some decisions must be made, but free will says that we can cut down the trees that separate the fork and build a damn road. Not understanding the tug to not go down that road, not understanding the butterflies in your stomach and everything else that says to not do something, only listening to the outside influences that have waged war with your soul for so long you have become almost immune to it. I know I have.

    I looked at my current situation and all I wanted was out. I fought everyone and everything that stood in my way. I clawed and I scratched my way until it almost beat me. I looked at my life growing up and I refused to allow my own children the same fate. At the time I thought I was doing what I was meant to do. Having all boys was a struggle, I am a woman trying to teach boys to be men. And I did the best I could, even laying the first bricks in their paths I thought they were destined to go down.

    Boy did that kick me in my teeth. I quickly realized that all those times I was fighting to be heard, fighting to go my own way, to do me, there was someone else telling me no. Saying I couldn't do this or that, that a girl didn't do those things, society wouldn't like for me to do those things, it's not how things are done, the bible says… Oh that damn book. Listen, I'm a believer, I am but for the love of all that is divine, stop throwing that book at people! Seriously! I was so tired of being told these things that I fought with every fiber to 'show them' that I could do and be whatever the hell I wanted out of pure defiance. I needed the reasons not the book. Context, structure, not filament and bindings. I had a conversation with myself, you know to get an expert opinion and all, and we decided that those boys would not be like other boys, they would not be like their mom. No, those boys would be better than that. They would rock to their own beat and do whatever the hell sets their soul on fire. So, I told them about the paths that they can take. Let them know that the trees in the middle could be a path they made, but that it wasn't the only path to take. That no matter what direction they went down, the consequences were different but that they had to own those consequences and decide for himself. That the choice was theirs, but to listen to themselves, to choose the path that resonates with their being, their soul. To walk to their own beat. Good advice huh? Yes well, I have been known to preach and not practice.

Nonetheless, they have done that very thing. I never tried to put them in a box, I have always allowed them to make their own decisions with the understanding that they own the consequence. My oldest was four years old when he came to me expressing his dream to be a Marine. At that age as a mother, we all tell them that they can be whatever they want to be, and I know some mothers that, what their four-year-old wants to be is not THEIR hope or desire for them. However, I was not that mom, and I am still not.

Being a different breed, MY only hope or desire for my boys was that they were happy and were doing whatever awakened their soul. The decision to allow them to be their own, to come into their own awakening, calling, afforded me plenty of resistance. Plenty of bible throwing if you will. I did not care, I was forged in war, and having kids made me an undefeatable warrior. I shielded and I fought for their right to do whatever the hell they wanted, to give the freedom to explore the soul that was given to them. To light the spark that was planted in them at birth. I never apologized for this aspect, for this I will gladly face my maker.

I waged war countless times against everyone and everything that tried to stand in the way of my boys becoming everything they were predestined to become, including against myself. In these battles I lost my own way, I forfeited my own becoming for them. A sacrifice I would do over and again given the choice. I noticed darkness creeping in from the back, but I did not falter. My work was not done making sure that no one or anything built that damn road for them. I stood against all the odds that one could face; some I would not wish on my own enemies. I walked behind them on the paths they chose, I picked them up when the fall was too great. They would look to me for advice, I would give it and end with *'the choice is yours, do what feels right, not what others deem right.'* I gave them every tool I had available for them to succeed in their own right.

That same four-year-old boy has a very old soul, I saw him the day he emerged from the protection of my womb. I knew then he was destined for greatness. That the soul that left one body and was lost looking for a home, found the same in my son. I believe that in him and his brothers. Each of them received the very soul that was meant for them. Each of them given the hardwiring to become. What I did not see was my own soul dying to save theirs. I did not notice that the trials and tribulations I faced as a child, as an adult, as a mother, a single mother, were detrimental to my own soul becoming.

I suppressed her cries and replaced them with weapons. Weapons I did not know would be fatal to my very existence. Weapons I thought were helping me on the path I was on. I did not realize that the paths I was on was not my own, but theirs. For that my soul suffered. You see this same response in people of trauma, in victims, in survivors. And I was all of those neatly wrapped in battle worn body armor. I refused for my traumatic life to affect my boys, and in my efforts, I am afraid it did. They saw what I thought was hidden, they endured what I thought I was shielding them from, they witnessed what I thought I was protecting them from. They rose above it all. They did not do it easily, or graciously, but they did for the sole purpose of becoming their own, of being better than I could ever be, of awakening their own damaged soul and healing it so that they could become one and grow into their own.

I have watched this manifest before me and I have been in awe of their fortitude. Of their growth. They were not resilient no not at all, they were resistant. Resistant to the outside forces that tried to shape them, they were resistant to the trauma that tried to break them, they were resistant to everything that stood in their way of their path to themselves. Learning this I realized that all along I was not resilient, that I too was resistant. It took me years of questioning, years of this tug of war with my upbringing and my becoming. Years of this psychic war that was waging in my person, to realize my soul was not just tired but extinguished. That the path my soul had fought so vigorously for was hidden under the overgrowth. The years

I spent fighting, running, denying, allowed for my vision to be non-existent. Just lost in a sea of chaos and darkness. A path no longer visible even in the daylight.

I have done the same thing repeatedly, expecting a different result, that I failed to notice I was slipping into insanity. I often asked myself,' *what am I doing wrong?'* Only to not find the answer to that question. I have slept without rest, worked without motivation. Just robotic aside from the constant battle of the boys. Now that they are all grown, I find myself lost in translation of what to do now and where to go next. Unsettled and uncertain of the life that lay before me. My purpose, my destination, my becoming, lay in the heart of the soul I extinguished, lighting others ablaze.

I have done things that I am good at and excelled in, I have even experienced things that made my heart skip a beat. I have seen things others wish they had and done things that others would never. All these things are just that, things, entities, check marks in a list of mundane that have done nothing to reignite a beautiful being that lay dormant in me. Not long ago I became sick, I started experiencing these crazy, weird symptoms. Saw, what seemed like, an endless number of doctors. All dumbfounded and stumped as to what it could possibly be. I won't go into details on this issue, but I will tell you that it left me in a state of wonder. Terrified wonder of 'what happens if?' I was afraid of leaving this world in the condition of my person, not my body, my person was in.

I started thinking "logically", robotically if you will. The warrior in me, the protector in me took control again and I began to discuss the options and outcomes, even before I had a diagnosis. I tried once again to lay a path that wasn't already made for me. The internal tug of war started again only this time there wasn't much of a struggle with my being, very little resistance. I didn't realize that this whole time I was depleting the very thing that needed me the most, the very kindling it needed to stay awake. I justified everything, I justified the trauma, the abuse, hell I even justified the justification. The one thing that would set me on edge about anyone else, I was doing to myself. I was allowing the light to go out, I was allowing the struggle, I was allowing the trauma to be inflicted. The whole time I was thinking I was breaking some sort of cycle, I was creating another one, and it had taken its pound.

You say, *'Oh Rachael, people who suffered from trauma, abuse, turmoil, it's not their fault. You didn't allow nor asked for these things to happen.'* The fact that I didn't ask for it does not mean I did not play a part in it. Let me explain this further. Our lives are dictated by the choices we make and the consequences we reap from sowing those choices. Now as a child we are at the mercy of our caregivers' choices, so those consequences are not in fact our own to accept, endure, or take as our own. Even though some do and carry that into their adult lives never following their predetermined path. I vowed to not let the choices of my parents dictate my path, I swore I was going to allow my soul to carry me.

In my efforts to fight that battle, I lost sight of the reason I was fighting, and I fell victim, if you will, to the consequence of that choice. I CHOSE to be with the men I did. By that choice I am guilty of the allowance that choice handed me. These words I am writing are my own. My own resonation and explanation of my becoming. I am not a doctor; I am not a professional of anything. I am simply a woman whose struggles scarred her into something new. If you have stayed with me thus far, you will see that very transition and hopefully understand.

On this path of destruction, I found that I was not alone in the chaos. I had babies, babies that were victims of my choices. And here we find ourselves in that cycle I so desperately tried to break. I suppose I did crack it some, as I, personally, did not treat or mistreat my boys the way I was, but I brought them into the chaos and hell I created by my own choices. In doing so, I created potholes in their paths. When I made the decision to say enough is enough, is when I saw not my life, but my boys' lives, flash before my eyes. In a Walmart parking lot during a very physical altercation with my youngest dad and husband at the time. They watched him beat, choke and manhandle their mom and little brother as he was wedged between he and I. They watched this man body slam their mom on top of their little brother as onlookers did nothing to help. They then watched their mom cry as police drove them away unsure as to if or when they would ever see their mom again.

Oh, but that still wasn't enough, nope, it was stupid close, the camel just needed that one straw. The straw came in the form of a phone call as I drove east on highway 7, a phone call from him requesting his precious shit that was in my car. I pulled over, screamed, got out of my car and threw his shit all over highway 7 and told him he could pick it up there. Right then and there, on the side of a dark and desolate highway I jumped. Feet first off, the damn man-made path and landed somewhere in oblivion. That was a hell of a lot better than the one I had been on.

I was told by one of my sweetest aunts, as I sat on her couch unable to sleep, unable to speak, to cry, just lost, that fate filled night, *'Rach, you are one of the strongest people I know, and you will get through this, those boys and you will be better for this.'*
Strength is not the absence of weakness; it is having the fortitude to endure it. And at that moment I once again silenced the screams in my head and prepared for the biggest battle I have, to this day, fought. I fought unapologetically, I fought irrationally at times, not listening to anyone, not taking anyone's advice other than the cries of my boys that night. This path I was on in that moment was paved in brimstone and fire. I woke demons that were dormant, I climbed mountains unsurmountable, never retreated, never backed down. I fought until the only thing left of that path I was on with him was my beautiful boy. I would be damned if he got stuck there as well. And so, I fought, forged in the fires that burned me, a hurricane wrapped in a tornado, I created another path paved in the ashes.

If you have yet to see the paths I have been on and created for myself, were anything but straight, righteous, dignified, or even correctly laid. The construction of them was lined with potholes, craters, volcanoes, and storms so fierce tornados are just puffs of air. Secured with hellhounds, their demonic keepers and chihuahuas (I have one and that little shit is evil and fucking crazy). Each one going its own direction, creating an unconquerable maze that even me as the creator, could not solve. All the while, the precious being that chose me to be her vessel, was waning, her light getting dimmer and her plans and aspirations for me were diminishing.

I started working out during all this, and I fell in love with the adrenaline and attention it allotted me with. I was hooked, forever on an adrenaline induced workout high. I craved it, it afforded me an escape from the war I was in, I loved the feeling it gave me. The sense of direction and I hatched another plan, or rather I found a path I once laid, in the maze of paths I created. I started looking into age limits on military service. Before my first born, I had a plan, I laid a path to join the Airforce, dead set on it, well not deadly I suppose as I was still a victim of my parental choices and very much NOT doing what it would take to be all I can be, wait is that Army?? Any who, nonetheless, at that time that was what I wanted to do. But trauma is the gateway drug and once that gate is open it comes with irresponsibility and diminished capacity, and here is where we bring in my first beautiful boy.

So, at the ripe age of 31 I decided, why not try again. Why not see if I can do what I set out to do all those years ago. Thinking maybe the reason I was feeling so lost was unfinished business. So, I swept off that path and started down it once more. I was committed, determined to make this one work. I shaped up, I worked out, I slimmed down and man I see photos of me back then and I was a different person. Unrecognizable today when I show those pictures to others. I was getting attention I never had before, and that alone fueled the high I was already on, dangerously so. I was still fighting the war with the ex-husband and that was a huge obstacle in the way of this path and my thoughts went dark. So dark that I am afraid that if I divulge it here, it will make you, the reader, culpable. I was unaware that revisiting manmade paths, in this case woman made, would darken the soul that was already weakened. Creating a sickness inside her that would, if at all, take years to completely heal from.

The thoughts that were rampant in my head, wanted to take control of my person and steer her into the darkness of black, and I was willing to let it. I was barreling down this path, unable to see past the tip of my nose. Oblivious to the ramifications, ignoring the outcome. On the outside you would have seen a mother who freed herself and her children from an incredulous fate, a woman fortified in strength and endurance. In reality, she was a facade to cover hate, an illusion for anger, a parlor trick for corrupted senses. Once again, I justified it, I justified it all. Some would see small cracks in the veil I so valiantly put up, and in those cracks a little of the anger and hate would spill out, and they would see. I would notice and I would quickly stitch the crack tighter than before. Never allowing anyone or anything to grab a hold of that crack and rip it up to use for cleaning cloths. Nope, my mind needed that veil, needed the anger and the hate, needed the illusion of it all. I was addicted to the trauma, to the negativity and all the attention the illusion was getting. I was lost and I justified it as free, happy, and settled.

I was 15 pounds away from the end of that path, 15 pounds and could not for the life of me get it off. I started working out twice a day, six days a week. Determined to get it off, unknowingly adding more muscle than dropping weight. I was frustrated and that just fueled that anger and I worked harder until those pounds became inches and those inches won me a seat across from a recruiter. I remember the looks I received as I walked, no I strutted, arrogantly, into his office. The same gentlemen were in there as when I walked into the office 6 months prior and 75 pounds heavier. The recruiter did a double take, literally. Never taking his eyes off me as I sat across from him, paperwork in hand ready to go.

You see I was still very much in a battle of control over my youngest with his father, even though the divorce was finalized at this point, he still tried to dictate my life by disrupting our son's. That recruiter informed me that I would have to give up custody to my children for the duration of basic training, temporarily. This is where I stepped on a landmine the darkness had placed in my way.

I heard the click under my feet and my heart sank as it exploded in slow motion. This meant that I had to allow someone to care for my children while I was gone, shouldn't have been a problem, right? I mean I had family, right? Plenty of people that would step up and care for them, right? Nope, not one person. There was a person, however, she was afraid that the ex-husband would come after her while I was gone and do something to her or worse, my boys. I could not put her on that path with me, even if it were a short stint of 8 weeks.

I nodded to the recruiter, took the form I needed to fill out, swallowed the tears, shook his hand and walked out of his office. I walked out head high and steadfast to my car, turned over the engine, cranked up the volume and screamed. You see I love heavy metal, and that was what was playing, so others would not notice that the screaming was agony. I don't know how long I sat in that parking lot, or even remember the ride home. I remember getting my boys situated from school, telling my oldest he was on brother duty and to order pizza and I headed out to the gym. I was there for three hours.

Working out is an excellent way to relieve stress, I now utilize it now, in this way but in a healthier way, because after the three hours, sweat drenching, powerlifting, heavy metal listening, work out I came home and ran for three miles. When I finally entered my apartment, I was no longer angry, but more determined than ever, I felt more powerful, more rage driven to stay on this war-stricken path.

Anger fuels many things, and we learn to use it for good, it can have healing powers. I had to learn in the most difficult ways, to use it that way. I had to realize the difference in rage and anger. I had to decipher and separate the two to recognize them individually. What I thought was 'relieving stress' at that time was actually giving more room for the rage to grow. The anger was subdued by the tumultuous workout, but the rage, oh the sweet rage, was only amplified by it. I found myself in a whirlwind of chaotic fire I loved. I welcomed this path all over again only now with a venomous fury. I talked to my attorney and was legally within my right to have a family member or anyone I trusted to care for my children if they abided by the custody agreement set forth at that time. Even though the ex-husband was trying to control me in this matter, the healthiest thing I did at this time was stop listening to his bullshit.

So, I set out to find a trusted individual, another landmine. Another 4-hour, rage filled workout, another plan obliterated. Ok so now what? Oh, look I found another path that was laid longtime ago, let's see if I can go that way now. This pattern of events spiraled violently out of control. Slamming into roadblocks like semis into concrete medians. I hit potholes, landmines, quicksand, you name it, I encountered it. Adding to my collection of shrapnel. Not once did I ever stop and say, *'ok Rachael, let's reevaluate this situation, let's turn inward and clean house, let's take a moment, a breath.'* Nope I did not, I justified it, I *'poor me'd'* it, I shook my hand at it, not ever taking responsibility for my part in it. Always the victim, never the perpetrator of my own device.

I slummed in it so much, I was used to the mud in my eyes. Used to cleaning my shit off everyone else and laying around in it myself. Used to the victim portrayed as a survivor, looking in the mirror and not recognizing who was looking back. The habitual,' I'm done!' was my go-to. Even though the words of my mother rang in my ears,*' when you're done, you won't say you're done. You'll just be done.'* I ignored her, what the hell did she know anyways, right? She was one of the reasons I am the way I am, it's all her fault, right? Habitually angry, addicted to the rage, and fueled by hate, and killing the very essence of my person in the mix.

I was so consumed by the trauma that was inflicted upon me, that I could not allow myself to heal. I would not allow my being to take control and transform me into what she needed me to be, so lost in the maze I created. Spiraling out of control, grasping at everything I could to slow it all down.

One summer day something changed, a spark flickered, just for a moment, enough to stir the precious being of my soul. I am a believer in soulmates and firmly believe they come in all forms and that we don't get just one, no, we get many, because we love many. This summer day, I felt him. I saw him and something inside me, so foreign that I tried desperately to fight it, damn near jumped right out of me. I saw him and did not understand the way he looked at me. Did not understand the magnitude of his being shining back at me. Oh, but mine did. He took my hand for the first time and a shock wave rushed through me, literally causing my heart to skip a beat. Electrifying every nerve, every fiber, lighting a spark in me I didn't know needed to be lit.

I had spent so much time in darkness, that light was foreign to me. For a moment I welcomed it, I did not let go of his hand, I never wanted to let go of his hand. I wanted to hold it forever. But the addiction of darkness had its claws in me so deep, it clawed and bit and scratched so that I would fight against it all. And I did just that, I fought against him, I fought his love, I fought his light, his electrifying touch, I fought it all. And yep, I justified it all again, always looking for the monster that would fuel the rage to feed the darkness. I was not prepared for his retaliation; I was not prepared for his strategic defense. I was not prepared for him. I was prepared for the worst, I was prepared to fight all the ugly, all the disturbing, all the chaos. I was not prepared, nor did I have any inkling on how to fight his magnificence. So, I did what I knew and that was to armor up and build a higher wall around the path that I laid and continue my destructive construction on it. Fighting his efforts to tear it all down, fighting his efforts to quiet the rage and calm the storm I conjured for myself. I wanted to run far away. Take my boys and my darkness and run. Forever in-flight mode, forever on that path.

Let me stop here and be a little technical, I know, I know, I said this wouldn't be one of THOSE books, but like all things, we need some clarity, and again I am not a doctor or professional, I am experienced in trauma. Trauma is not an entity that can be forgotten, erased, or gotten over, the definition of trauma is *a deeply distressing or disturbing experience.*

A deeply rooted, prolonged experience is the most detrimental of the traumas. Abuse in any context, witnessing a death, witnessing or being a victim of a heinous crime, all these extenuating circumstances set a stage for destruction and when one was forged in it, actually bred into it, they know nothing else. Their version of love, their version of healthy, is so warped and clouded that when they are presented with a different version, they see it as wrong. Or at least I did. I cannot speak for anyone else.

Trauma is an entity that must be met with the right amount of love, fortified strength and just enough patience to even begin to heal.

He had all those traits and then some. He could have said, *'fuck this, you're damaged beyond what I want to deal with.'* I'm almost certain he thought it a time or two. But he stayed, and he fought. He fought for the soul that was dying inside me. His being recognized that mine was suffering, he saw the carnage that was my person and he wanted to heal it. The problem with that is that the notion of one wanting to fix and heal someone who is broken is a battle never won. You cannot 'fix' people. You can help steer them, you can love them, you can show them there is a better way, a better path, but the choice has to be theirs. You can help clean up the wreckage of all the paths they made, of all the destruction their storm caused, but you cannot force them to walk their destined path that lay underneath it all. No matter how much we want to, we must let them do that on their own. It does not belong to us, for we have our own.

   He tried to and oh how I love him more for it. His efforts caused many arguments, many sleepless nights, many second guessing what the hell are we doing? He never, not once gave in to my shit, never faltered, stood his ground. Me, as stubborn as I am, met his every move with a vengeance. He wanted to marry me, he wanted to let me be me, he wanted me to lay down my sword and take off the armor and rest. He wanted to take the reins and allow for me to heal. I saw it as he wanted control, he wanted his way or no way, he wanted to take over my life and I would be damned if I let anyone ever do that again. So, I fought him all the way to alter. True story.

   I was aware of something happening in me, but I was clueless as to what. I remember standing in front of him holding his hand, looking at him looking at me. I remember our friends and family gathered, fading into the background, I remember feeling the same shock I felt that first meeting flowing from me to him and back again and the tears flowing from my face, ruining a shitty makeup job, again true story. Confused as to this feeling I was experiencing, it was so incomprehensible to me that I stuttered my vows and as I write this, those same tears are burning my eyes. That feeling that was taking control of me I now know was love. Pure unadulterated love. Love so profound that I did know even know it was healing the wounds I suffered. That it was slowly putting me back together where I was obliviously broken.

    I watched him see me, see into my being, I felt his being touch mine and I wanted more. I felt the electricity cauterize the festered wounds, I felt them scab over into beautifully crafted scars. Each telling a story, but none, able to be broken open again. That moment forward I never wanted to be without him, I needed him, I craved his touch, his love, his person. That night was one of the best nights of my life, it was the epitome of perfection. I was surrounded by people I loved, but that did not matter, I was in the arms of a man whose soul matched mine. Had I known what was to come after, I do not think I would have let my guard down so easily. That wonderfully constructed night would turn into 6 months of pitch-black darkness, plummeting that feeling of euphoria and love into quicksand.

    My world came crashing down, and a bomb was dropped into the path I was now on, with just one phone call the very next day. News that haunts my dreams to this very day. News that forced me to suit up once again and quiet the newly awakened being. News I do not wish upon anyone. That very next day, I had to go identify my brother's dead body. A night and a whole day a casualty of the darkness. One that awoke Rage once again, and she was pissed. She seduced the darkness and gave birth to a new hell in me that Satan himself wanted no part of. One I had to share with my beautiful aunt, who did not deserve to witness something, but did so out of her love for me, for my parents, and for my brother. She is not forgotten in this, but this is not her story, and I cannot tell it.

    Once more a path laid. One of unimaginable pain, chaos, spiraling out of control so fast, my head was spinning. I spent the next 6 months or better a shell of a person. I lost a child 18 years prior to this, lost a grandparent shortly after that, but none of those losses touched the magnitude of losing my brother. It cut a new wound so deep that even the love of my husband's being could not heal, despite all his efforts. It was a piece of me that died with him, a piece that for so long was my protector, my savior, my friend. He was not your average big brother, you see we were forged from the same fire, although his did not burn him the same way mine did, he watched the flames consume me and he did whatever he could to put them out.

    My rage filled anger took over and she was hell bent on running the show. She found words that she never knew she had, and she spewed all over the ones she felt were culpable in my brother's death. The path she forged was laced in an inferno fueled with all the stages of grief rolled into one fat ass blunt. One she filled her lungs to the brim with its smoke, not caring who the casualties of this war would take. The old saying, *'hell hath no fury like a woman scorned,'* is nothing compared to a rage filled grief stricken sister. I was not prepared for this path, I did not lay this one myself, but I did finish it. My brother's death was not at the physical hands of any one person, no. It was at the mercy of his trauma. Of his upbringing. I will not go into the details of that as he is not here to tell it. I will say this, he often spoke on what he endured growing up that led to his darkness taking him. And here is where I took over that path. Veering off the one that was meant for me, one that was healing and preparing me for my destiny. I lunged, sword first, into that fire willingly. I swam in its lava filled waters and I welcomed the chaos it gave birth to.

Rage took over and set up residency; she had no intention of leaving. She was set on waging war eternally. She destroyed everything in her path, good, bad or in between. Only pausing when it came to my boys, and even they saw her destruction, felt the heat emanating from her. Everyone around me kept their distance, not wanting to be burned, not wanting to get in her way. Even though I still craved my husband's light, his touch, his love, I no longer wanted it. That notion only fueled Rage even more. I didn't want him touching me for fear it would subdue the rage and hurt I felt. I wanted to feel this, I wanted it to burn, I wanted it to take me. He did not back down, he pulled away, but he did not relent, not one time. I did, I veered off the path and took up construction of the one that ended my brother's life. I allowed the outside influences to dictate Rage's orders to her. I did it all.

Rage inhabited my being, made it her caged prisoner, I can still hear her screams and cries. I can still feel the pain of the wound it left. She violently exploded on my husband when he would complain about my pulling away, she would attack my children and bonus children unmotherly so that they too were afraid, and I justified it all. Call me the queen of justification. Looks like I am literally writing the book on it. I gave my husband an ultimatum, because you see, he too had some shit that I took on, that weighed viciously heavy and just made Rage ecstatically stronger, and well I had my own shit to deal with.

Not knowing that my shit was affecting my children, but I did see that his shit was and I wasn't having any part of it. I know, so hypocritical of me. Rage colored eyes sees not hypocrisy. At the time I was blinded to anything rational or logical. So, I told him I was leaving and that he could come, or he could stay, that I cared not what he did, and I did just that. I ran. Two states away, I ran. Thinking this was the way, being led on by Rage's vindictiveness.

Two states away another beautiful being awaited my arrival, one oblivious to the plans of the rage brewing inside me. That rage did quiet down some, she did find some rest, but not enough to set free the being she locked away. That rest would be short lived when my husband followed suit and he unwillingly packed his chaos up with our house and set up shop in our new home. Our path of marital bliss was beginning to flood and be destroyed. The beautiful being that was waiting for me two states away had her own hell as well and being the empath that I am, Rage inhaled deeply, letting all their shit to become mine and exasperated her rule. I now found myself at a fork in the path I created. Wait, what? How is there a fork in a man-made path??? My guess is, divine intervention, a damn earthquake shattering the road, splitting it into two pieces.

I began to feel trapped, like a rabid dog in a cage. Gnawing at the bars, foaming at the mouth, that I was losing sleep, I was pacing the floors, crawling on the walls and out of my skin. I couldn't keep a job, I couldn't think straight, I couldn't function properly. Arguing was my way to do anything, that and crying. I did not know anyone could argue or cry so damn much, and yet I caused a flood of salty animosity. My only escape I thought, yep you guessed it, was to run. Seeking solitude and redirection I ran as far north as you could possibly get in the United States. I ran to the unknown, to the fastness of cold and terrain, I ran. Looking back, I did not see all this as running or escaping, no I saw it as a solution, a way out, a survival technique. It was not until later that I realized I was running, always stuck in flight mode. Unsettled, unhinged, and unpredictable. A very dangerous combination, an explosive array of a sickness driven path.

In the very Northern and as far East as you can go in the good old USA, I met Silence. An entity I knew existed, but one of legends told. I met him raw and unadulterated, and I was forced to listen to him, no matter the resistance in which I tried to overpower him with. I was forced to sit with my rage and my hurt, I was forced to sit down on the very path I was on and listen. Listen to screams echoing from my being. I was forced to listen to the storm raging inside me, an ever enduring, never quieted, thunderous storm. I was forced to listen to all that pain silenced with duct tape and super glue. I was forced to recognize that the inferno was burning me internally as well as eternally.

It was when I could hear it all that I noticed my soul was tired. There are different concepts of tiredness I have learned. There is physical exhaustion, there is mental fatigue, where your mind is exhausted from thinking and feeling and then there is soul tired. This type of tiredness hits you differently. It is a tired that if not acknowledged it could be fatal. Not in a sense of death, no, but in a sense of being lost forever, there are far worse things in life than death, and this untreated tired, is one of those things. It is here when my symptoms increased and the unknown of what was wrong with me sank in. It was here that while listening to Silence, I realized just how exhausted my person was.

    I dove into myself, listening to what she would need in order to come alive again vibrant and whole. Although I knew the damage she had endured would not put her back as she was before, I knew that healing her wounds internally would help me heal my wounds externally. I knew that the path I was on was not where either of us could heal on. When the path is not oneself, it cannot mend or heal what it destroyed to make it. I am a firm believer in predestination as I have stated throughout these rantings, I was just lost in the flames of the external forces at play, including my own. Blinded by their flames and waiting for the smoke to clear so that I could see.

    I checked out a book once from the library, and at first, I had trouble reading it. Not because it was incomprehensible, but because the words that flowed from it, hit me square in the face. I felt like the author was talking only to me. That he reached into my person, touched my soul and wrote what he found. I put it down more than once, only to pick it up and read it in its entirety in a single day. Something I had not done since I was a teenager. I read it and re-read it, it resonated with me so profoundly, that as I sat with Silence, I bought it, and I studied it. Applying its words into my life. Learning from its pages, I started to let go, I started to heal. This has not been an easy journey as we have seen in these pages, and they only tell an edited version of it.

I am half Native American and my whole life I have been indoctrinated into the Southern Baptist faith and all that that belief system tried to instill in me. I have always questioned everything, including these teachings. Always wanted to know why, know more, thirsty for knowledge. Never getting the answers I seek, only plummeted with the 'Good Book'. I have never been drawn to that belief system or any organized religion, but I have been drawn to the ways of my ancestors. This is not to say I do not believe, I just believe differently, I afforded myself the title of an Omnist, which is someone that sees truth and guidance in all teachings and religions. I have always wanted to know more, to learn more about how all ancestors lived. I begin to seek my own truth, my own belief system if you will. I started listening to my soul and affording her the overdue attention she needed, and I deserved.

I was far from completely being healed, far from the exuberant self-love I needed, but I was now set on the path predestined for me. Not one of anyone else's making, nor my own. One determined by the very being that sought out my vessel for her home. She had a lot of work to do and in order to do that, she needed her light. One that has all but been extinguished, mostly at my own hand. Where do I get such a light? That I cannot answer, for it is different, I believe for everyone. As for me, I am still learning. I am taking my experiences, my trauma, my rage, my anger, my hurt and my pain and I turning it into lessons. Some of which I did not teach myself but learned from others.

I flew out to California Thanksgiving of 2020 to see my son before he deployed. I carried with me the burden of my illness and the struggles I was facing with that and still being a mother to my youngest who was dealing with his own struggles at that time. It was during this conversation when my beautiful boy looked at me, locked his eyes with mine and said, *'mom you have to stop. Stop with everyone's shit. You have done what you could do for the boys, for me, for everyone but yourself, you have to stop now and take care of yourself. We will be ok, but you, you have to stop.'*

In that moment, I realized that what I thought I hid from him, that I thought I shielded him from, I did not. He saw it all, he saw every tear, every blow I took he felt, every pain filled sleepless night, he did not sleep as well. It was then I broke a little more. Not in a bad way, no, What I learned from silence was that it was ok to break and let it go that which did not serve me. And letting go and allowing my son to see me did just that, it broke off a piece I had no use for anymore. Never really did. He saw right through my shit and called me out on it. Now that is my boy. I took his words home with me, and I planted them deep into my person and allowed my soul to swish them around in her mouth and really taste them.

I realized I was not being selfless when taking care of everyone but myself, but I was selfishly denying myself that same care and I believe it literally made me sick. I talked to my parents about the illness that was looming over me and remember my dad telling me that I needed to take care of myself, gee where I have heard that before. That it was NOT selfish of me to put myself first. That I was no good to anyone, including myself, if I did not in fact let my soul rest and heal. Beginning to see a pattern of intervention here. The funny thing is none of these people were discussing this in a room together with anyone else where I was planted center stage. Divine intervention? Most likely, but that is a topic that I will not get into here.

My husband and I decided that we needed to head back south and maybe seek answers elsewhere as the medical personnel I encountered in Maine were anything but forthcoming or willing to help. Borderline negligent and incompetent if you ask me. So, we did, we took the 1700+ miles from Maine to Kentucky and set up once again in the same area I ran from a year and a half previous. A part of the path that I did not have any reservations about. I have come to understand that while on your journey to becoming, if you are met with any resistance at all, it is not the path you need to be on. When I was not met with any resistance in this move, nor hesitation, I knew I was in the right direction. This man of mine, I have often said that I am so surprised he is still with me. He would tell you that he is a glutton for punishment, and well that may very well be true, but his soul matches mine and that my friends, is love divine.

In this transition, I noticed that the beautiful being that was waiting for me in Kentucky that her soul matched mine as well. She is the other light I needed to set my soul ablaze. I did not feel the gravity of just how much so, until I was in Maine, until I could not see her, or could escape on adventures with. She too was what my person was longing for. I believe that soulmates come in various forms, I believe that a soulmate is not singular but plural and that we need each of them in order to maintain the path predestined for us. I believe soulmates complete the circle of one's coven.

Back in Kentucky, my oldest deploys, the world was thrusted into chaos with a plethora of unknowns, and I found myself in mom mode once more, of pure agonizing turmoil with the unknown. He has deployed before, but this one was different. I felt it to my core that it was gravely different. I soon realized that it was not the situation that struck me, but the unknown. I fell into a depressive state and my soul once again suffered. Only this time I fought back. Thanksgiving 2021, funny how it's the same holiday that my boys find it ok to call mom on her shit.

My middle son, a no nonsense, no bullshit talking, dude, comes for a visit. He sat in my living room and told me unprovoked, *'mom, the first thing I noticed is your house is dirty, I have never seen it this way. I look at you and I see you. I see your tired mama, I see you. You need to stop,'* (hmm this sounds familiar),*' you need to rest, you need to quit worrying about James' shit, my shit, you need to stop it. If Isaiah were here, he would say the same thing.'* Oh my beautiful blunt boy, he did. Little did he know his brother said those very words to me a year previous on the exact same day. He did not know that his brother said that to me and was not at all shocked that he did.

You know when you hear something once you go ok cool, I can see that, but twice, you need to listen and learn. I did just that. I listened to them; it took me a minute, but I did. And I put my foot down, washed my face and listened. I climbed out of the stump I was in with the current situation of the deployed kiddo, with the direction my life was headed, and I started. I knew I wanted more, I knew I

needed more, that my soul deserved more. I knew that I was beyond ready for my becoming. I knew I had work to do, that we had work to do. I knew that I couldn't do it alone, I knew I would need help. But first I needed to let shit go. I needed to forgive everyone that ever wronged me, I needed to 'mommy kiss' every traumatic booboo, most of all I needed to forgive myself. I needed to heal the damage I did to myself. I needed my person to know she was ok, she was loved, she was beautiful, she was wanted, and all those things needed to fuel the spark, to set it ablaze so that she, I, could burn so bright, the sun needed shades.
I needed to connect myself to myself, I needed to become.

"Sometimes letting things go is an act of far greater power than defending or hanging on"
- Eckhart Tolle

2

"Each of us has myriad possible incarnations that exist in the eternal present moment, all waiting to be discovered.'
- Joe Dispenza

    You may be reading this going, but Rachael how did you do it? And me being a fuck around and find out type person, that's how, that's my answer for everything. I did a lot of trial and error and I continue to do so. I am in a constant state of progression. Not a work in progress, but a success in forward projection. I was stuck and the first time I felt myself move; it sent a wave of electricity through me. Just enough power that I started shedding this bent up, rusted out armor one piece at a time. The weight of all that I have survived, overcome, went through; that shit is heavy and even heavier and harder to get rid of. I started with putting the sword down, for my arms were shaky and weak. I stared at it a while, watching it as if it were going to move, contemplating picking it back up again. When you hold on to something for so long, it becomes a part of you. Intertwined in your skin, so connected, so real that letting go is no easy feat. It is you, and even the slightest upset to its grasp, burns so deep you learn to leave it alone. Never realizing that it is slowly killing you.

I did not realize that holding something so heavy was causing me so much pain, so much anxiety. Not until I put it down. Not until I watched it at my feet, looking at it wondering why in hell did I even have to have something so vile, so corrupt. Why did I enjoy the poison so much? I noticed that the poison created an illusion of protection, a magic trick of safety, not knowing that at the same time it was pumping death through my veins, that it was leaving a trail of rot and disease.

As I contemplated, I discovered that the *why* didn't matter. It was irrelevant. Not a part of my path, but a part of my past and needed to be left there. Worrying on it, trying to figure it out, prohibits my ability to change, to grow, to shift. So, I kicked it, watched it slide across the floor, leaving sparks in its demise. I watched it skid so violently, I felt the tear from my person so vividly that it brought tears to my eyes and made my knees weak. I wanted to run after it, catch it, feel its weight again, but I couldn't. I couldn't allow myself to hurt myself anymore. I needed to stay the path of forwardness, of change, of progress.

Addiction comes in many forms, we often associate it with tangible, visible, outwardly, entities of control over oneself. We see it all too much, it's familiar and customizable. What we don't see are the internal addictions that made the deal for the external addiction to show itself. Again, not a professional, just an addict. And in order for me to understand that, fully and completely, I had to understand the soul's addiction as well. The very one that started from a very young age at the hands of those I was supposed to trust, those that were supposed to protect me and keep me from harm. That took root and grew into a demonic tree of chaos and turmoil. One that I had a part in feeding and watering masked as 'protection'.

It all comes back to choices, as a child at the mercy of others, I did not have a choice in what was done to me. It was done so regularly that it became the norm. I thought that everyone treated their daughters this way. That the product of my raising that was me, was how it was supposed to be. I can't remember when I decided that it wasn't normal. That it wasn't right. I reckon I always had a notion or a feeling that it wasn't, but to pinpoint the exact age of it, alludes me. As a teenager I rebelled and I rebelled hard, so maybe that is when. Here we introduce the outward signs of trauma, of a wretched path of destruction.

The actions of others, the choices they made in the most influential part of my life, created an effect so powerful that my vision became warped and my thought process. Giving birth to that sword, my escape, my 'savior', drugs. The details of this are lost and gone. I do not remember my early teen years. That path I forged, no longer visible. Just a craved notion that made my salivary glands active. All I know is I did not stop. If you ever had the privilege to know me as a teen, I was high. Didn't matter what it was, I did it. Came easier than I thought, because well my brothers too had trauma, free stash was the best stash. So, when anyone reminisces with me about those times, I just smile and wave, because hell it's probably true.

What I do remember is my 17th birthday. Coming down off of a binge, trying to appear as normal as I possibly can in front of family as they celebrate my annual existence. I remember thinking about my cycle and when exactly was the last one. I took my twenty-one dollars I received every year from my grandparents and took my dad's truck and off I headed to my friend's house. I don't even think I knocked on her door, must have, her grandmother would have strangled me if I didn't knock or speak, but that part is hazy. Anxiety mixed with coming down, not a good source of recall. I went into her room; she was sitting on her bed painting her toes. That I remember because the smell made my stomach turn. She looked at me and all I told her was get dressed and come with me to the store. She did not hesitate. We sat up shop in her bathroom armed with two pregnancy tests, and all I remember next is her screaming in my ear shaking me as we watched both portray a positive outcome. Ever had morning sickness chased with withdrawals?

   Motherhood slapped me in the face with a shovel. One that set me on a path of withdrawal and not recovery. *Oh, but Rachael, getting clean is recovery!* Nope, it is merely expunging the poison out of your system, recovery is healing from that. Two very different things.
Getting clean was not a choice. There was something bigger growing inside me that I could not harm. Pumping that poison through my body was my choice, this being inside me did not have a say and I knew I had to speak up until he did. Getting clean gave me a new piece of armor. Are we getting the picture on this? From that point on I kept adding piece by piece until I was completely covered in the weight of reinforced steel.

Now dawning this armor did have its perks, I went on to graduate high school, attend college, earn a technical degree and have two more beautiful baby boys. I did so not for myself, no, for them. I did everything for them. As a mother should I suppose or that's how it's supposed to work, right? Now don't get me wrong here, having those crazy, dirty, amazing boys, I would not change one damn second. I just now had to reinforce my armor more with each of their births, and with that it became heavier. Looking at them now, hell I must have done something right.

Not a day went by that I did not want the poison I so loved to pump through my body, especially when the weight of being a single mom was too much to bear. Not one day I didn't want the escape, just for a minute. That's all I wanted was a minute of numbing, of destruction. So another piece of armor was installed. I never stopped adding pieces. Each one designed for its specific role of what it was covering. Its specific duty and command. Each one heavier and more reinforced than the last. I would label them as strength, healing, courage, power, etc. Never understanding that just because you call dogshit ice-cream it's still dogshit, and still eat it.

I created another addiction, an addiction disguised as strength, as all those labels I put on each piece.

Putting the sword down was my first step towards recovery, actual recovery, actual healing, actual strength. I did not realize at that time that my want of those poisons started to fade, the need began to quiet, the desire began to starve. I was afraid that the feeling I was feeling was illusory, that it would run its course until I could get another fix. I was afraid to take off more, but that is the beauty of courage, isn't it? It is being afraid but having the strength to do it anyways. I did not run after that sword I kicked, no, I watched it fade away into oblivion, never to grace my calloused palms again.

I looked at my hands, I ran them over each other. I felt every callous, cracked every knuckle, traced every line. I ran my hands over my arms and caressed every inch of them. I wrapped them around my body and felt the cold steel that housed my chest, grabbed with both hands and pulled as hard and as violently as I could. I could not get it to come loose. I tore and I clawed and through tear-soaked eyes I fell to my hands and knees. Defeated. The sword was so easy, I didn't understand. I heard a voice tell me to try again, but from a place of forgiveness. Huh? What? Forgive who?

You see the chest piece protected my heart, my lungs, my vital organs. All those things needed for the body to survive, I wrapped it in cold hard steel about ten feet thick. The heaviest piece, the hardest to get off, to give up. The control I disguised as strength. The piece I am to this day still working to completely shed. Something so heavy, so thick, doesn't just fall off. No, it must be carefully chiseled, so as to not damage the precious cargo it holds. From a place of defeat I stood, dusted off my hands on my legs and heard the clanking sound of hollowed metal being stuck.

Our legs carry us through life, both figurative and literally. We walk, run, skip, jump, our way through it all and in battle we take a stance, ready to fight, feet planted, legs spread, ready for enemy advancement. I was no different, always in a constant state of fight or flight. Makes sense that I would add armor there too. Makes more sense that I would take these off next.

Running seemed to be my specialty and I don't mean doing a hundred-yard dash or cross-country race. I mean when the fight was too thick, the enemy too strong, or I needed a change of venue to continue the fight, I ran. Ran from everything I did not deem 'good for me'. In that I ran from just that very thing. So used to running shit myself, that any outside source of help was deemed tainted enemy scum.
We all read earlier that running was my expertise, so I will not go back to that. I will move forward with this. Someone once told me that facing the enemy head on, meeting them on their playing field, was better than trying to lead them into a trap. I never understood what that meant. Face them? That is all I have been doing, right? What the hell did they know anyways?

   In my mind's eye, I was doing that very thing. I was fighting, I wasn't taking their shit anymore, didn't care who it was, and I was fighting, on my own terms, my own field, my own business. I was showing them, wasn't I? Showing them that I didn't need anyone to help me, I didn't need help at all. Yeah, I am sure you have figured out how well that worked for me. But in my defense, I did own up to being the queen of fuck around and find out. Each time I ran, I added more armor, more weight to be carried. I did not fully grasp the gravity of how much, until I took the leg pieces off. One by one I unhinged them, letting them fall to the floor, the sound reverberated through my body and shook my core. The legs left underneath were bruised and battered, weak and shaking, I collapsed once again to the floor. Rolled over and laid there staring up at the heavens. Legs screaming with infuriating thanks.

I sat up and ran my hands down each of them, feeling the muscles that hardened from the weight. I thanked them for their support, their loyalty in carrying so much and never giving into the weight of it all. For enduring it all. I massaged the bruised and battered pieces and stood. I stood taller, I stood braver, I stood solid. I picked up each piece one by one and threw them as far as I could. I watched the universe grab them in midair and they exploded with such magnitude the blast was deafeningly silent. I stood there a moment in awe of the release. Hypnotized by the relief of letting go of so much weight, mesmerized by the powerfulness of my soul healing.

I no longer want to run; I no longer feel the desire of endless battle. I welcome the challenges and I allow their resistance to change me, to shape me into someone that doesn't need the smell of the battlefield for motivation. I take each challenge as an opportunity for growth and direction. I take each problem as already having a solution, I face it head on. I get help when I need it and I am no longer carrying it all alone. My beautiful best friend and soulmate tells me all the time that I am not superwoman, and well she is right. I am not. I am just a girl on a path. One she did not create herself, one she welcomes with open arms, resources, family, and friends. One that does not go without issues, no, as we are all human, outwardly anyways.

We don't even know how much weight we carry in our arms and our legs until we set it all down. Until we look at the carnage on the floor and take inventory of the heap of shit laying at our feet. Placing it all in their perspective piles of manure and taking account of everything. We carry so much and some of us don't even have enough arm length or leg muscle to handle it all and it spews all over the place. Like glitter. Just going to let that sink in a bit. The wreckage strung all over the floor, in a chaotic cloud of volcanic ash, infecting the spaces and people in close proximity. Burning some to the point of unrecognition, or at least that is how they are seen. They are so tired of being in the wake of chaos that they remove themselves from it. Forever seen as 'different', 'barely recognizable.' to the one who burned them. I did that very thing with my brother, oblivious to the ones I did it to.

When I saw myself, really saw myself all broken, beaten, just raw nakedness, I was appalled at first. Disgusted at the image portrayed before me, ashamed even. I was taken aback by the sheer audacity of the life I lived. But then I looked, really looked. Beyond the bruised and broken parts, beyond the scars, beyond what my life tainted eyes have allowed me to see, and I saw what laid underneath it all. I saw myself. I saw the person under it all. The beautiful being with her arms stretched out welcomingly. I saw Rachael. I asked my husband if someone asked him to describe me, what would he say? He just looked at me, oddly, puzzled at such a question. Most would describe characteristics I have, like smart, pretty eyes, outspokenness. But those describe my character, my looks, not my person. *'But Rachael, aren't those the same thing?'*

I don't believe they are. Your character, your occupation, your looks, do not tell the story of your person. They do not describe your soul. Those attributes afford you the desires or lack thereof, of others. The description of your soul can be told by your soul's connection to the outside world. Some call it your aura, others the way you glow. I say it is your eminence. What I saw when I looked beyond all that smoke and mirrors, was a being so vibrant, so magnificent, that I struggle to find the words to describe.

I saw a kaleidoscope of light that shines so bright, they could hide darkness for good, but welcomes it in her embrace. I saw all my paths that led to the right one, paint a picture so painfully stunning, I couldn't help but watch it. I found the calm to the storm. I am beautiful chaos, forgiver of all that was broken, lover of all that was tarnished, acceptor of all that was lost, in me. My character just reflects that. I was so blinded by the trauma, the addiction, the struggle, that I could not see what was right in front of me.

If you were to ask me now to describe myself, I would start with my characteristics, sure, but I would elaborate and accentuate my eminence. I used to say that I danced with the devil, and he hated when I would lead. Now I say, I welcomed the dance because it taught me that even when faced with horror, the light in me still shines. That the acceptance of oneself is not for the righteous, but the disenchanted. To be able to let go of the pain, the trauma, the burden, I was able to pick up the pieces, restore in my being the willpower she needed to take my hand and lead me down the path I was destined for. To allow my eminence to break through. I am my person, and she is me.

I sat down all I was carrying, I let go of all that I was dragging around. I shifted into becoming. Although I am not fully, completely there, I am finally able to take on what that very thing means. I could not accept myself as myself, I was constantly in search of someone else. Someone molded and shaped into whatever box I created. Not ever, even once, considering that there was no space for anything I could put in it. But I damn sure tried. Misconstruing every aspect of being, of becoming. Excusing every heinous atrocity. Yep, justification queen at your service. Not taking responsibility for my role in that destruction. Holding onto others' responsibility for the same. I sat it all down. Some I threw so hard, so far, I did not care who it hit as long as it hit in the right general area. I got rid of all that no longer deserved my attention, that did not serve my being, that diminished the flame in my soul.

    I started listening to the being inside me. I started. I did not become a born again anything. This is not a tale of addicts of old. Nope. This is me, raw, naked, exposed. This is something that I am sure will piss some people off, and this is me unapologetically not giving a damn. I am not here for the comfort of others. I welcome all opinions, that does not mean I have to accept them, or incorporate them into my life. I cannot control other people's tongues, minds, or attitudes, but I can control how I respond to them. The very first thing I noticed about this shift; is how quiet I became. I always had something to say, whether it was warranted or not. Always talking, always vocal. Now I listen more and respond less. I have always been an observer, but I observe more now. I have even noticed this shift has upset others in its wake and that speaks volumes about them not me.

    My dad has told me that you can hear more when you shut the hell up. Always thought it was his way of getting his chatty daughter to be quiet. Now I see, it was his way of telling me that not all things warrant or deserve a response. That is powerful. Majestic even. What was even more prolific was the epiphany I had when I found out he meant that included myself. We are our own worst critic and enemy. We sabotage ourselves more than anyone else ever could. Myself included. This goes back to allowing shit to happen. Allowing dictatorship over myself at my own hands. As much as we are our critics, we are our own master. The problem with this is the fact of too many chiefs and not enough indians.

   Let's go back to the beginning here for a minute for a refresher on this. I believe that our soul is not our own. We did not create it; it was gifted to us. It chose us as its vessel. Our outside influences try to manipulate into what they want it to be. Constant bombardment of sentiment, instruction, dictation, until it relinquishes control and succumbs to it. The soul is still the soul, just now the body and mind are in control and the soul, the essence, is lying dormant. When the outside source has exhausted their efforts, we take over, we become accountable for the upkeep of the influence. We drown out the cries from our being and continue down the path that was laid for us, wreaking havoc to the very thing that gave us life to begin with.

   I was definitely my worst enemy. I would constantly replay and repeat it repeatedly to anyone who would listen, myself included, to all my justifications, all their faults, mine included, so much that I would do it in my mind as I tried to sleep. Never telling myself to shut the hell up, forever on a mission of self-torment. I did not realize how much I spoke, how much I carried on relentlessly about everything and nothing at all. Holding my words as gospel, until one day, I just stopped. I simply ran out of shit to say. I noticed that I was on a continuous cycle of rinse and repeat, with everyone, myself included, and it was fucking exhausting. Just absolutely draining both physically and mentally. That led to me discovering my exhausted soul; so, I listened to my dad, and I shut the hell up.

    I began with quieting the words I spoke aloud, just let others speak. Only offering to break my silence when cued or prompted. Really taking in what they had to say. If it takes a turn to a cycle of rinse and repeat, I politely steer it into a different direction, or I shut it down completely by excusing myself from the conversation or I simply stop responding altogether. This too has caused upset of others, and this too has brought me closer to becoming.

    I then put into place boundaries, I will go into detail, you have to figure out your own boundaries and listen to yourself by shutting the hell up. Boundaries are necessary, I believe they are essential in awakening your person. I feel they are needed to heal. They are to be respected by everyone, including yourself. I had to learn that the hard way. FAFO queen still! I could not put a boundary in place and not have myself honor it as well. It simply does not work that way, trust me I tried.

    How can I tell someone I don't like the way they treated me and put a stop to it, when I do it to my damn self?? I mean seriously. The boundaries had to be put into place for myself. I had to stop the influence and manipulation I did to myself. Easier said than done for sure. It is not a light switch you turn off, or a line you draw in the sand. It takes commitment and courage and the right event to do so. I did not just pull boundaries out of my ass and was like, oh this looks good let's put it here. No, I had to articulate the perfect one.

My favorite, insert sarcasm, is the one I crafted to not be so judgmental of my body. To welcome it as a beautifully designed work of art. It housed and brought forth three beautiful baby boys, produced an angel. It has carried the burden of motherhood and withstood all kinds of storms, trials, and tribulations. I need to constantly give it praise, love and admiration. In placing this boundary, I have also added a branch to that one and not allowing others to negatively impact my body as well.

What some think is a joke, or even think they are helping, if it upsets my person, I remind them of my boundary. I tell them I do think that what they have said or done is helpful, fair, or good for me. I no longer stand for allowing anymore detriment to come to my person. Either by my own hands or those of others. This too upsets others and I still don't care. If what I do or say to protect myself from harm offends you then you deserved that. That tells me that there is something in you that accepts the boundary I put into place, but the outside influence of your person doesn't. I have come to recognize the difference between the two.

I have stood in the mirror or laid in bed at night telling myself everything that I am everything I thought I wasn't. I must. Becoming starts within. You cannot glow outwardly if inwardly you are dark and desolate. I immediately address all outward discrepancies as well. I don't hold onto words that were meant to be spoken. Holding in words that were meant to be spoken are poison in and of themselves. Fatal to everything. Release them when needed, when warranted and never out of anger. This too is easier said than done.

    I do not claim to know anything at all, I speak only from experience and what is working for me. I cannot speak of anyone else. I can only allow my story to be told, in my own words and voice. If in return it helps someone else, then so be it. I hope it does. Writing these words, laying all this out here for the world to read is difficult but therapeutic. I have searched so long to find my words, but I had to be quiet first. I had to listen to hear. I had to stop making so much unnecessary noise and just listen. One of my favorite things to do is listen to classical music after a workout. Not just any classical but either piano or guitar. There is something so soothing about the rhythm of the music that just calms my muscles and nerves after a workout. What I noticed was I was not hearing the melody; I was listening to the feeling it sent through my body. The calming, relaxing, quieting, feeling.

    I do not speak while listening to the music, I do not take in any stimulus, I just listen. And that is the epiphany I was talking about. I had to learn to listen to the rhythm and melody of my person, I had to quiet all other stimuli and listen. When I was able to do that. I heard what she needed. I heard what needed to be said and what didn't. I didn't only hear, I comprehended and then I implemented. In return, I became more. More than I was, each time I go quiet, and I listen, I am more. With more, I can write these words, and with more, I can release them. In a constant game of quiet and listen, never the same outcome, always in a forward projection of progress and acceptance. This, my friends, is the epitome of healing, at least for me. It started with me shedding the weight, getting rid of it for good, then shutting the hell up and listening to what was needed to heal from the weight of it all.

The words once an addict always an addict I believe is a false sentiment that leads to recidivism. I am not the labels outside influences have given me, I am not the mistakes I have made or the product of a raising. No. Once I shed it all, once I started listening to my being, I found I was never a victim of circumstance where the trauma sunk her teeth in me, but more. Destined from the very beginning for more. I am bruised and I have been broken, but I am so much more than the scars. So much more that I will no longer say I am an addict. So much more that I no longer say I am an abuse survivor. No, those things are what happened to me and not what happened FOR me. They do not define my person, they no longer determine my path, looking back, they never did.

"My transformation represents more than what is just skin deep; it represents my motivation, drive, and willingness to constantly improve."
- Jinder Mahal

3

"Everyone can rise above their circumstance and achieve success if they are dedicated to and passionate about what they do."
-Nelson Mandela

    I have a tattoo of a Phoenix on my right calf, a forever reminder of how I rose from ashes into something more. And just like the Phoenix, she is forever changing. Each cycle she rises more beautiful and more extravagant than the last. Her eminence radiating so brightly you dare not to get too close, but so welcoming you can't help not to. I only strive for that radiation. I don't want anything less for myself. Always changing for the better. Always evolving. Failing and rising, better, brighter, more. I am beginning to love the life I am living. I count the blessings every single day. I am embracing my person more each day. This does not go without any failures, setbacks, or struggles. No, it comes with all of the above. The difference is now that I am fully invested in my predetermined path, if I start to stray, I am quickly brought back, and we begin again.

This has allowed me to do things I have never had the balls to do before. To seek horizons, I thought that were too far to reach. It has allowed me to be unapologetically me. All the way around and allow others to see what I hid under all that armor. To see the raw nakedness of my person, that I was too afraid to allow anyone to see. I have weeded out those that did not serve my person, those that did not accept my quiet and my change. I have rid myself of negativity including that of which I inflict upon myself. When a negative entity in any form surfaces, I quickly disperse it. I light sage, I say aloud, no negativity can enter this space of my person or surroundings only positivity and light. I found what my being wants in order for her to thrive. She is me and I am her. I do not allow anyone or anything to disrupt what I have put into place. This includes myself.

I am still human, outwardly so, I have faults, I have struggles. The difference is I recognize I am responsible for the outcomes, no one but me. I welcome challenges that push me forward and even more so those that don't. I no longer need to fight alone, I have help and I have accepted that I am only one person and not superwoman. I do not take on anyone else's shit, I allow them to keep it. I offer my silent listening and my warranted advice and nothing more. I hear her, I see her, I love her. She is me and I am her. It has to be this way, I cannot see, hear, or love another unless I do the same for my being. I have learned what she needed to reignite, and I supply her fuel to infernally burn daily. Every morning I wake up and I thank her. I thank her for getting through the day before, and every evening I thank her for a job well done for the day. Each day is a day closer to totally becoming. Each day I am closer to fully embracing oneself. Each day I forgive myself.

   Forgiveness is never guaranteed. Unlike trust and respect, it is not earned the same way. Forgiveness is an outward expression to heal an inward wound. I was not ready to heal the wound I created myself and let fester. No, I was not ready to take that responsibility. Not until I listened and felt the pain I inflicted. Not until I heard her cries. It then only did I crash and burn and begged for it. And I still did not embrace the depth of forgiveness. Not entirely. I did know that I could not forgive anyone else until I forgave myself. They say forgiveness for others is not for the one being forgiven but for the one forgiving. It is so much easier to forgive someone else than yourself. You never want to see that you need to forgive yourself for what others have done to you. Yes, I said that right.

   You have to forgive the hate of yourself, the destruction, the sleepless nights, the storm that wreaked havoc. The allowance of it to continue raging. You have to forgive it all. You are only in control of what you do, your response to a situation, your choices. And I did that very thing. I carried around the burden of the trauma, I did. The one that inflicted the trauma does not give a damn about how it affected me, if they did, they would have never done it to begin with. I had to forgive myself for that. I could not give it back to them, there is not a rewind button or a magic wand that removes it from me and gives it back to them. No, there is only forgiveness, and when it is done correctly, removes that burden effectively and completely.

I have a lot to forgive myself for, and every day I do just that. I forgive myself for the thoughts I had of those that damaged me, they did not deserve a place in my mind. I forgave myself for believing the lies they told me to control me, I forgave myself for the warped sense of sex I have of something so beautiful. I forgave myself for myself. Only when I am done forgiving myself, I can start to forgive others. This growth has impacted my life so much, I can sit in a room with my mom, I can see her, and all her complexities and I can understand the trauma she inflicted because she, herself, was stuck in her own cycle of rinse and repeat. I can allow her to see me and see that I did not succumb to the addiction of her trauma. Forgiving her will come, I am sure of it. I first must forgive myself for the hate I had for her.

Forgiveness is a daily admission that I am becoming, that I am healing, not just recovering. The scars are fading and one day I know they will be completely gone. I know that I could not have done this alone, and I forgive myself for thinking I could. My oldest sent me a text recently for Mother's Day, *'Happy Mother's Day! Hope you have an amazing day. All that you do, does not go unnoticed, you are appreciated, and I am grateful for you.'* Forgiveness of myself for thinking these beautiful creatures were just another product of a raising. They are most definitely not. Forgiveness of myself for ever thinking I was a bad mom. I could go on with what I need forgiveness of myself from, but that might need to be another book, maybe.

    I no longer fight the dark, I welcome it. I know it never lasts long, and that the beauty of the dark is illuminated by the moon. Forever lighting it until the sun shines again. In the dark I do the most forgiving, it is a great place to shed the ashes and become new the next day. It is a place of unknown, a blank slate ready to be written on. Each night casts shadows of the day, and I can clearly see them, forgive them and welcome them into the light. I accept every part of me, good, bad, or ugly. I know what needs to be tended to and what I need to do for that very task. I listen to my body, I hear my person, and I trust my mind, to do what is needed to continue this adventure, to not be afraid of this path.

    Wherever it may take me, I excitedly take every step towards it. It has opened so many doors and put in place many others. It has afforded me the fortitude needed to heal. Healing is not a band aid you rip off, no, it's a slow weaning. I welcome the process. No matter how painful, no matter how dirty, I welcome it. I allow it to happen. I willingly take whatever is needed to heal, to grow, to forgive, to continue to move in a direction in tune with my soul.

    There is another tattoo I have of a compass, and it says *in the waves of change we find our direction.* It is as true now as the day I put it on my body. If we cannot change, we cannot grow and if we don't grow, we become stagnant and nothing good comes out of stagnated water. Change is never easy, and I do not know a single person that says.' *Man, I love change, bring it on, it's my jam!'* Not a damn one of you. If you say that, you're lying to yourself and others.

It is necessary in order to move forward, or any direction for that matter. It is essential to not be stuck. I do not like anything that disrupts what I call my organized chaos. My room may look a hot mess, but I sure as shit know where everything is in it. I notice quickly when something has moved or changed. My husband thinks I am a crazy fool, neurotic even, perhaps, but the point is this, change is upsetting, and I have a rule that I applied to my mothering of three boys. If it doesn't challenge you, it won't change you, and excuses prohibit your ability to change.

   I never allowed my boys to even consider excuses or dismiss things because they were hard. So why do you ask, did I allow it of myself? Hmm, hell if I know. I am figuring that out as we speak. I will say this, I had to start practicing what I preached. I had to mother myself for lack of better words. I must tell myself daily this very rule. But first, I had to accept change, I had to not fly off at the handle because my husband took his book off the bookshelf and put it on his own shelf. You get the point. I had to accept that I only control my response to situations and that in order for me to grow, I have to respond accordingly.

   I must change. So, I welcome each days challenges in hopes of the change that I can grow from. Constant momentum. That change starts with forgiveness. Change is an evolutionary concept, foreign even. A complexity even in the word. The very definition is the act or instance of making or BECOMING different. Why the hell would anyone want to do that? I mean we are comfortable being who we already are right? Umm, no I am not, and from some of the conversations I have had with or heard others talk, neither are anyone else.

I can only speak for myself, the rest of you can figure that out. I can say that no I was not comfortable in my situation, status, life or whatever you want to call it. I was far from it. I was not in a state of comfort, my life was not rainbows or soft fuzzy socks, nope it was sandpaper toilet paper and quicksand. So, change I shall, and it started with the acceptance of my human side, the forgiveness of my being, and the power of my soulmates' help. People who truly want what you want, your soulmates, will do whatever is in their power to help you execute whatever is necessary for you to change and grow. They want to bask in your glow and you in theirs. It is a match made from the galaxies, that only gets stronger with motion, and motion cannot happen when you are stuck. A body in motion stays in motion. Simple physics really. I guess, if um, physics could be simplified, sure. Nothing about this process has been easy for me. Necessary, yes, easy, nope.

It is difficult to let things go and not pick them up again, then it is to revert back to them. It is easier to stay stuck than it is to keep moving. I knew a guy once that was helping me the best he could literally ten thousand miles away with my weight loss goal when I tried to revamp the military path. He said something to me that has stuck with some ten years later, *'no matter what, keep moving Rachael. If you have to slow down, slow down, but don't stop.'* At the time I applied it to my workouts, my running, now I apply it to everything. I hear his voice in my ears telling me this over and over. This didn't just apply to my physical sense, but my spiritual sense and my becoming more.

I have come to the conclusion that when I stop, I sit, and when I sit, I am closer to the floor where I laid all that shit down. Now I know that willpower comes to play in this scenario so save your eye rolls for one second. Let me explain, that statement my friend said literally spells out willpower. Having the fortitude to keep going, to not stop, is will power. I rest when I need to and I listen, always listening, always in a state of forward progression.

Always changing no matter how challenging. The hardest obstacle, the one I started with first, forgiveness, is one I have decided will be a constant fate of my evolution, so I decided to have side changes if you will. After I looked beyond the limits of my mind and body, I began to love all that I saw. Every curve, every blemish, every piece, I loved. Some parts need more loving, and I give it to her. I do not work out for the looks or the weight loss, that is simply a perk of doing it, I do it because it provides part of the love to my muscles, my veins, my heart, that my body needs. I do not do anything anymore for the perks it provides me.

My motivation has shifted to that of becoming more, more than labels, more than stereotypical innuendos, just more. Along the way I get better, I get healthier, I get the perks. It all started with forgiveness. Each day I do some self-love, each night I burn it all down to be new for the next day, better, stronger, healthier. I do not claim to know what I am doing; I just know that this is what is working for me. I cannot tell you what will work for you as it is yours to own and do with as your soul sees fit. I can offer some sort of resemblance in the fact that we all are human, we all have been through one thing or another and that my story is no more or no less tragic than the next. The issue is what we do about it. Do we stay stuck on rinse and repeat, or do we get out of the damn shower?

Where I am on this journey, is where I need to be. My soul, for once, is coming alive each day. Each day I come closer to being. I do it with dignity and grace and I do it because it is vital to my existence. I was put here for a reason, and that reason is slowly, but surely, revealing itself to me. I may have been born into darkness, but I am pure light. I have fought long enough, have let go of the heaviness of the sword and leg armor. What is left is this chest piece and my helmet. The chest piece gets chipped away each day I forgive, each day I burn it all down and set anew the next. The helmet is heavier to lift and even harder to let go. I have to conquer the depths of my mind, the far corners of sanity and dance with the insane. A fortress forged of barriers and protective coatings of gray matter.

The problem lies with the mind's ability to protect itself from itself. Makes this part of my path harder to navigate and even harder to conquer. I have been having dreams of things I need to unravel and expunge from the depths of my subconscious. I am often terrified and awaken in the night into the safety of my bedroom next to my husband, my safe place. When they started, I would not go back to sleep, I would just lay there replaying it repeatedly, like a broken movie reel. Analyzing it frame by frame. Just stuck on what happened and the what ifs. Now I go back to sleep, understanding that dreams are our mind's way of dealing with subconscious issues. Not intended to be interpreted but finished and resolved so that that area can heal completely, erasing it from memory.

There is a difference between forgetting and putting it out of your mind. To forget means that it can be triggered to be brought forward and disrupt the path you are on, to put it out of your mind, means that it can't be triggered again. That that area has been healed, forgiven, and a new memory took its place. You still remember it; you're just not affected by its sting anymore. It poses no more threats, no more trauma, nothing. It is accepted, processed, and let go of. I have found that my dreams help me do this very thing. I dream of my brother, and before I would wake up in tears, never falling asleep again after that. I have not fully healed from his death, but the fact that I am healing from it, has allowed me to not have a tear-soaked pillow when I wake up.

It is a beautiful way for me to see him again. It is a way to deal with the hurt I experienced that night, one that will never go away, but one that can heal so that I cannot be triggered by, just from the sheer mention of his name. I am able to write these pages for everyone to read. I can sleep at night not afraid of what lies waiting for me in my dreams, and I wake the next day safe, secured, healthier. Security is a term often used in place of safety. These are two different beasts. Two beasts that fight over dibs on my personal growth. I am safe in that I have a sense of awareness when I am out alone somewhere, I know what to do in an emergency, and I have a 38 special, six shot revolver that daddy made damn sure I knew how to use. That is my safety. These things do make me secure. Security comes from within. I have never felt secure in my own skin, remember when I said I never felt like I belonged anywhere, well that is my insecurity rearing her ugly head. I did not fit in anywhere, I was in a constant state of just existing, taking up space. Always looking for my sense of self.

My husband can calm my storm with just one touch. In his arms is where I want to be forever. I love his essence, I love how his soul touches mine in the most provocative, seductive, loving way. He is my security. He saw right through my bullshit, saw my person, saw my soul, and he touched it. Started its inferno and danced in the flames. When you can lay everything bare, and find that he didn't run for the hills, that is security. When I started to see what he saw, to feel what he felt when he touched me, to really be comfortable in my own skin, then I was secure. Looking at myself naked and exposed, I saw where I belonged. I felt the warmness of its touch. Security comes from an awareness of oneself and accepting that awareness as whole, as just, as beautiful. It is a consistent effort of love and admiration for myself, a constant forgiveness, a constant acceptance. I accept the me that is I. I accept every flaw, every aspect of her. She is me and I am her. I am becoming, I am changing, I am growing.

My growth is in constant motion. Sky's the limit kind of mentality. One that this path I am on deems it necessary to continue to do so. Looking back, I'd like to say that I was growing this whole time, but it was an illusion I constructed to keep me going. To keep me existing. A sore spot on my psyche for sure. I am often saying that experience is the best teacher, but just because you learn something does not mean you grow from it. Case in point, high school algebra. I can't tell you a damn thing about it, I learned it and it didn't grow into anything but a headache. Even now just thinking about linear equations makes my head spin. I learned a lot of things over the years, some of which I think maybe something small, sprouted, but not to anything of any significance.

Experience in things has been both positive and negative. I learned to be a dental assistant, loved it, had the opportunity to advance in that field, never had the desire to. I couldn't envision myself any further than where I am now. It was a means to an end, a way out of a bad situation that I allowed to happen. So now, in order for me to grow, I must leave that experience where it lies. A great outlet should I ever find myself in need of anything materialistic, I can always hop back on the tooth train. I do it now because I want to, and I do it when I want. This freed up space for me to grow, for me to flourish, for me to do something I know I will grow from, write. I have tons to say, an ocean of words I can construct into a masterpiece.

An element of mastery I have no experience in at all. Unless term papers count or essays in school. I can sit down at this computer and spill all my thoughts, pour it all out, lay it bare, grow from the therapeutic rhythm of the keys, getting lost literally in translation. I adore words. Their beauty and power speak volumes. I love when it rings truth in your ears, when it moves your soul, speaks to you and only you. The written word, so intelligible and almost tangible, I just want to hold in my hands and let it run through my veins. I get better with every keystroke. I welcome the change it is affording me; I openly accept the growth these pages will bring me. I do not write for your pleasure, but mine. If I touch you the reader in any way, thank you. Thank you for allowing me to move you, to speak to you, to help you grow. I see you as I walk along my path.

    My path is that of my own, no one else's. If these words that I wrote here reach you in any way, thank you. I do not write for recognition, just the ability to do so is enough for me. I wrote because it helps me grow, it helps me navigate my path. This path is not laid by my hand, no, it was pre-laid for me, directing me, guiding me, growing me into becoming more. My husband and I will answer I love you, with I love you more, I now know that it does not mean that he loves me more than I love him, it means that we love each other beyond that of ourselves. Our souls love each other, our paths merged into one another, and we are becoming more together. We were not meant to travel this path alone. I cannot see any future he is not in. Somewhere along the way my path merged with another and hers into mine. We may grow separately, but we do so together. Her path is her own and mine my own but running side by side the whole way.

"In one lifetime you will love many times, but one love will burn your soul forever"
                                  - Unknown

"Having a soulmate isn't always about love, you can also find one in a friend."
                                  - Unknown

4

"The ship is always off course. Anybody who sails knows that. Sailing is being off course and correcting. That gives a sense of what life is about."
-Michael Meade

   Where I am today, is not where I want nor need to be. I am not enlightened; I am not sailing on the wind of opportunity. No, I am merely navigating through life, but with a little pep in my step and a new sense of direction. The right direction. I make every day count a little better than the last. I have come a long way, learned a lot of things, re learned some lessons I missed and still have room for more growth and improvement. I no longer look back and wonder 'what if' or 'how come?' No, if I look back, I am thankful. Thankful that I was not consumed in the fires I created, thankful that I was not eaten alive by the very beast I gave birth too. I am just thankful for it all. There are still things I need to let go of the chest piece that has been hardest to shed. But it flakes off a little at a time. Writing this has helped me to shed a big chunk of it, and if this helps anyone else, then I thank you for breaking another piece of it off.
   I was walking with my best friend yesterday and I love our walks and our talks. Sometimes it is indeed the same

conversations we have discussed time and again, and sometimes that can get a little redundant, but each time we both bring a new perspective, a new way to handle whatever it is we are needing at that time. We do not bring the other down or try to out sob story each other, we listen, we engage, we learn, most importantly we grow. I have walked alone too much in my lifetime and walking with someone is very strange and at times uncomfortable, but I have come to enjoy that strange uncomfortableness. Learning to be quiet when necessary and speak when appropriate has taught me many things. Not only about the person I am talking to, but about myself.

I have learned that not all things deserve or warrant a response. I have learned that sometimes someone just wants you to listen. That concept is not foreign to me at all. I have often found myself where I stop talking in a conversation or I don't talk at all, because I wasn't looking for an answer or commentary, I was looking for a sounding board, someone to just catch the words I had to throw out of my mouth and head. I have treated people how they have treated me and that I have learned is very reactive and not responsive. Now I work on treating people responsively. Some behaviors I have encountered would warrant my anger, but not my reaction, and I have given both. With growth, I have learned to exhale my anger and inhale my compassion.

A lot of times people aren't mad at you, but themselves. I have lashed out at people for that very reason. Just needing to make someone as angry and hurt as I was. That is just not how I want to do things, not anymore. I honestly don't think I ever wanted to do things that way. It is exhausting and takes up too much of my time. Time that I could have spent doing something that makes me happy. Redirecting that anger elsewhere. I am not saying I do not get angry or that I do not lash out, I am, after all, still human. I am saying that when I get angry, I have a better hold on it and when I need to vent, I vent, I get it off my chest and out of my head, and I move the hell on. What is different is the response I give myself. Do I belittle myself? No, I don't, not anymore. I thank myself for not getting out of control and doing something or saying something that I can't take back.

   I am thankful for every opportunity. I welcome every challenge, and I honor every set back. Why? Because it is too damn heavy to carry it any other way. Walking with my girl, she was venting about something that was said to her that just crawled all over her. No, I will not tell you what it was, her privacy is my privilege not yours. She has been upset about this for some time. Each time I have seen her we talk about it. I do not tell her, *'Dude what the hell, this again?!'*
No, I do not, I listen to her, I let her get whatever it is she needs off her chest. Then I offer suggestions. I never give unsolicited advice, but I will suggestion the hell out of you. Just saying. I told her that the next time this person says something like this to you, you should tell them, thank you. Thank you for showing me how I do not want to treat people. Thank you for showing me how my growth has affected you, this means I am on the right track. Thank you for letting me see just how stuck I was in your presence.

I have a phrase I like to use; I stole from a song although the name eludes me. I tell people if I offend you, you deserve it. No I do not mean that I offend intentionally, no, it means that if what I say, do, or don't do , offends you then there is something in yourself that my path intersected with and disrupted. It means that it hit a nerve under your own armor for whatever reason and it is something you need to fix in yourself. Most of the time what I say is not directed at any one person, nope, a hundred percent of the time it is my own offensiveness that I call out. Yep, I call myself out on my own shit, who better to fix it than me. However, if my person calling out my shit offends your person then, shoe, lace, wear.

I have laced my own shoes plenty of times, some of them way too damn small. I have worn them just because I am too damn stubborn to take them off and deal with the issue at hand. I have learned through this transition on how to do that very thing. On how to not even try them on. They are too expensive for one and not my style for another, and I absolutely hate buying shoes, so why do I want to wear some that are too tight, too small, or too offensive. Makes no sense. I would rather walk barefoot and let the earth's vibrational pull fill my soles with energy and abundance than be cramped into an ugly, dusty, offensive shoe, someone tried to throw at me. I mean seriously!

So, stop being so damn touchy. I say that with love I truly do. I have to tell myself that daily. I am a mother of three boys, a wife, and everything that all that entails, so getting offended has come quite naturally to me. I have had to learn to just leave it where it lies not pick it up, I have had to learn on how to determine why it upset my person, why I allowed it to affect me in a way that half the time it was not even meant for me, but again, I was offended so I deserved it. So, I have to fix what it was that made it offensive. This has been challenging to say the least. It has made me accountable for a lot more than I am willing to admit, but it is necessary for my growth. If I continue on this predetermined path, it is necessary for that progression.

When I find out what it is that offended me, I can figure out the why and that means more healing, more pieces of the chest piece falling off and more air filling my lungs. Breathing gets easier and easier each time. I cannot tell you the last time I was able to take a deep breath without pain. I had gotten so accustomed to the weight of the armor; I didn't even notice I was suffocating under it. As the pieces fall off, the air that fills my lungs is harsh and cold. Icy sometimes even. The armor, still heavy in the areas it remains, and each inhale an icepick is driven into my lungs.

Breathing brings in needed oxygen to the brain and organs supplying them with vitality and life. It also allows positivity to enter while exhaling negativity and when there is struggle to do either, the pain can be debilitating. Each time I inhale I take it a little deeper, the deeper I can take it the more I can exhale. The more I can exhale, the more negativity I can get rid of. Growth, healing, change, is not easy, not comfortable, not free, it is hard, painful, necessary, and the result is magnificent. I am not there, I may never get to the end, but I will continue to push forward, only looking back to give thanks and honor. I will lose people along the way; I will gain them as well. Most importantly I will find myself, I will get to know my person more and more and I will have a firsthand account of her success, of her growth, of her healing. A witness to the witness. She is me and I am her.

My goal is to not have a goal. Wait? What? I don't know how many times I have said 'oh I want to do this, or I want to do that.' and I set a 'goal' to only either not even start or stop a quarter of the way through. No, I no longer make goals, I make deadlines. *Oh, but Rachael aren't they the same thing??* Nope. Goals are set with an end game. A habitual cycle of rinse and repeat, hence New Year's Resolutions, and we aren't on that cycle anymore. Deadlines have an end game. Have a solution, that becomes a revolution. The definition of revolution is to bring about CHANGE. Recently I was offered a chance to go somewhere I have never been before. An opportunity to see an area of the world I never thought I could possibly reach. I did have a want and a goal to see this very place, sure, but never did I put anything into place, nor did I have a deadline.

I kept seeing the advertisement for this trip constantly and well I believe in signs. So, I reached out to the coordinator and was like 'you what do I have to do?' I got an email and I looked at pricing and I did more research, and I told my husband,' I'm going to Ireland!' He told me if I can find the money, boom, a deadline! A goal would have been ok, let's save this money so I can go, and we all know that when we save something always happens and we have to dip into that to use it. Well, I found the money and I did it without disrupting anything I needed to do in the meantime and that included an unexpected expense of fixing my rust bucket of a car. Ireland, here I come. The first time I have ever been out of the country, popping the cherry on my passport.

So that is what I am doing. It has helped me to be more focused on my path, more determined than ever to get the things I want, to live the life I deserve and to have a hell of a time doing it. It is a long overdue compliment to myself. I owe to myself to have a healthy mindset to meet the deadlines I set. I don't go to the gym, because I want to lose weight, no, I go because it affords the health, I need to sustain my life. Why not have that same mindset in every aspect of my life. I have done for everyone else, neglecting the very basic cafe of myself and I am sure you have seen or got the gist of what else I neglected.

You cannot grow in the same clothes you were lost in, that is not how it works. You have to shed those tattered, dirty, clothes and wash your ass. I have a lot to wash, it is going to take time for me to be the clean I want and need to be. Some of what I have to wash I did not soil, and that is even harder to cleanse. Like I said, growth is disgusting, but necessary. I was stuck so deep that I thought it would consume me and take me to the depths of Haiti's, and it almost did. The decision I made to shed the armor did not come at my own device, no, I had help. Help that I fought, help that I ridiculed, that I dismissed as having ulterior motives, help that kept coming for me like a swarm of bees until I caved under its sting.

I thought the help was going to harm me, I found out it hurt me to heal me, to correct me, to help me get on the right path. I can tell you where I would be if it weren't for those that came into my life or re-entered my life. I can tell you I would not be where I am today, nor headed where I am going. They choose to grow with me and not against me, while still growing on their own. That my friends is love, pure, unadulterated love. I have found myself in love with them more every day. Yes, you can be in love with a friend, especially if it is your best friend, your soulmate, as well as your significant other. Love is a multi-universe of abundance. One I used to only have for my boys. My sweet, crazy, drive me up the wall boys.

Staying on a path that is not one I intended for myself is not easy, it is hard work every single day. I am learning myself for the first time. Taking on new experiences and senses I had no idea I had or could do. I am witnessing a change in the mirror, and I am liking what I see. I am feeling the spark between my husband and I again, I am healing an angry mind, I am listening more and speaking less. Mostly I am loving honestly and not out of obligation. I stay when I want to run, I say no when I am exhausted and need me time, I say yes more to things I would have felt guilty for doing. This is all growth, this is all healing, I am experiencing brighter days, even though I look back to darker ones. Growing doesn't mean you forget where you came from or what happened to you, it means accepting that part of your life and moving on and allowing the universe to heal you.

Allowing the air to fill my lungs and nourish my body with a flow of forgiveness, gratitude, direction, and life. Living intently, unapologetically. Not standing for injustices to inhabit my space, not allowing negativity to consume me. Taking every obstacle from this time forward with fervor and grace and hitting it head on. I still have sleepless nights, but those too are waning. I still have struggles, but each day I am thankful for them for making the right kind of stronger. I welcome the night into my soul and allow her rest, I awake each morning wanting to see those that I share a life with and not feeling pressured to do so.

Obligations are met that sustain life, bills, food, etc., but I no longer love out of obligation, I no longer feel I have to do something for my family at the expense of myself. I am no longer responsible for anyone's shit who is over the age of wiping ass and making meals. I am only responsible for myself. My duties as a mother will never end, but I have used my authority and delegated my kids' shit and my husband's shit right back to them. I cannot help anyone if I can't even help myself, and that is what I am doing from this day forward.

These words I wrote in these pages have been difficult to say the least, and maybe when I have healed some more, I will put that into words. They have been therapeutic and have helped me grow even more. This path I am on is my own, not by my hands but by my becoming more. I honor all those that have set me up to fail, mistreated me, misused my trust and abused my own honor.

I thank you for showing me how not to be. I thank you for allowing the strength needed to withstand your blows and advances. I thank you for not filling up my love with your hate so that I can have room for the abundance of love I have now. I thank you all. I do not condone what you did to me, your treatment of me, or your wickedness, I do forgive myself for accepting what you did as my fault, as who I was, as my path. My prayer is that you can forgive yourself for the same. In time I know I will forgive you as a whole. That is the whole reason for this growth, for this change in me.

"Forgiveness doesn't excuse their behavior. Forgiveness prevents their behavior from destroying your heart."
-Unknown

5

"Nothing is real or a lie, it all depends on the color of the glass you're looking through."
                                                 -Manny Trillo

    Through the looking glass I go. On a new adventure, with a fresh pair of eyes. I will drink from the cup I have poured. I will do what sets my soul on fire. She is anxious to burn brighter. I want her to burn so bright the whole world can feel her heat. I have things in motion, myself being the main train. I am excited to be on this path, I welcome the gravity of it, I want to explore every nook and cranny of it. Take it all in, hold it in my hands, smell its sweet aroma. Every day is a new and exciting adventure I can't wait to wake up for and every night is more restful than the last.

    The challenges that lie ahead, I welcome with honor and await their obstacles with amazement of what they might be. I am ready for the bewilderment of change. I may never completely reach my becoming, but I hope that when this body is done and my soul searches for her new vessel, that they continue on this very path she has laid for them. I hope they let her burn bright and fierce and honor the light she gives off for them. Until then I will do that. I will honor her trust, fuel her light, and I will graciously await her next move. I will not move with her direction.

Listening with every nerve, every vein, every piece of this body she chose to continue her journey in. Battered and broken I may be, but nonetheless grateful for the shit I endured that brought me to this place on my path. I will be forever grateful to those that wronged me and even more so for those that didn't. I hope you, the reader, can understand this sentiment. I hope these words I have written here moves you in some way, or maybe not, but I thank you for reading and if you didn't throw this to the side at first glance and stayed with me to the end, I hope you took something away from it all. Maybe it is simply an understanding of where I came from, or maybe you know my story on a more personal level, either way thank you for walking the small part of my path with me.

I thank you for your story whether it is told or not, I thank you. I hope that you can one day do the same for someone else. That is forward progression and not a work in progress. You may look back and see the darkness, but I hope you honor it, I hope you see the light that lays ahead and welcome it. Love both, cherish both, honor both. For both were you and you were both.
I regret nothing of my past and I regret nothing of what this path I am on may bring my way. I accept both wholly because I could not have one without the other. I cannot grow if a seed is never planted. Don't stop, if you have to slow down, slow down, just don't stop. Don't stay stuck, every movement can motivate the next.

These words may never reach anyone at all, and that is ok too. I needed to say them, to see them on paper to rid them of my brain, to heal and to grow. If they never reach anyone, they reached me. They told me about myself, held me accountable for my shit. They made me realize how much I was carrying around, how much pain and sickness. They afforded me the courage to allow you, the reader, a glimpse into my darkness. I am stronger in a good way for these words. I am now ready for whatever comes next. I am ready for the unpredictable, for the trials, for the happiness, for the adventures of this path. I am ready to feel the inferno of my soul and give her whatever she needs to burn it. She is me and I am her.

    I am not at the end of my journey, no, I am at the beginning. Still raw, still hurting, still healing. It is a story never ending, but I will leave you for now. For me to tell you more, I must heal more. I must listen more, talk less, and be more. For now, my being is but an ember of a fire, I work daily to send her flames roaring towards the inferno I know she can become.

    If I have learned anything at all on this journey is to travel light and embrace the ride in what ever may come. Facing things head on has become my way of continuing to move forward and not let things get under my skin. If they do, I don't let them stay there long at all. I encourage you, the reader, to do the same. Let it go, live your life, do what sets your soul on fire. I have to remind myself of this very thing every single day. I am not a work in progress, but a forward progression of success. I am not my trauma, nor the abuse I exhibited upon myself. I learned that what has been done to me, did not happen over night and what needs to be done will not either. It is a day to day, sometimes minute by minute excursion. Mysterious in its expectations and I wouldn't have it any other way.

'The life in front of you is far more important than the life behind you'.
        -Joel Osteen

"There was nothing her soul loved more than the moon, because even though it was always going, it would always come back. The moon, because even in its shrinking and growing, its waxing and waning-there was never any doubt that it would be full again. '
        -Kimia Madani

"Pay attention to your patterns. The ways you learned to survive may not be the ways you want to live. Heal and shift."
        -Dr. Thelma Bryant- Davis

"I dedicate myself fully to my purpose. I embrace the path that leads me towards my desires. I open to the magic that flow in my veins. I am grateful for the intuition that guides me forward. I trust in my own unfolding. So, it is."
       -Ara

"We are addicted to our thoughts; we cannot change anything if we cannot change our thinking"
       -Santosh Kalwar

"Forget about enlightenment. Sit down wherever you are and listen to the wind singing in you veins. Feel the love, the longing, and the fear in your bones. Open your heart to who you are, right now, not who you would like to be. Not the saint you're striving to become. All of you is holy. You're ready more and less than whatever you can know. Breathe out, touch in, let go."
       -John Welwood

"May we stop seeing ourselves through the eyes of people who never saw us."

-Shane Steele

REFERENCES

30 BEST QUOTES FROM BECOMING SUPERNATURAL BY JOE DISPEN
 Kenneth Wong - May 6, 2021; The Millennial Grind

60 BEST LETTING GO QUOTES
Steven Mueller

126 TRANSFORMATION QUOTES
Lisa Mills

BLUE LIGHT NIGHT
By Rachael Hinkley

"There is no love like the love for a brother. There is no love like the love from a brother."
                    -Astrid Alauda

   Mike, your demons are gone now, may your light shine in death as your million-dollar smile did in life.
                    Love Always, Rach

Blue Light Night

1

Cold. Ever been so cold that it seeps into you like fire in your veins? It numbs you from the inside out, wrapping its icy fingers around your heart and throat, dumping a cube of ice in your gut to sit and wreak havoc on your insides. That is the kind of cold that only recently began to thaw in my soul. A cold darkness that settled in one January night and I doubt will ever completely leave.

New Years is supposed to be a time for renewal, resolutions, and revolutions. A time, we all deem the 'right time ' to change, the perfect time to start something new, but for me it was definitely a time to change. A change I was far from prepared to experience, a change that sent me on a roller coaster of starless nights. I hate roller coasters. Let me back up a bit and tell you about the events that led to one of the darkest and longest nights I have ever experienced, and I pray I never experience again. A month prior I received a phone call, one I had all too often received, late in the evening and I was annoyed at it. I had a long day at work and was not in the mood for whatever shenanigans this person needed or wanted from me. Being the person I am, I answered. A scruffy voice asked me what I was doing, and I begrudgingly responded with,' *nothing, I just sat down from cleaning up after dinner, what's up?'*

"*Can you come pick me up?'* He asked. I let out a rough sigh and looked up at the clock on the wall. It was 9 pm and I really did not want to. I asked from where and he gave me directions. He then asked if he could stay at my house as he had nowhere else to go. I told him it was fine and that I would be there to get him shortly. I grumbled under my breath as I sat the phone down. My husband, who was my fiancé at the time, looked at me quizzically and I rolled my eyes and said, *"My Brother needs a ride, and wants to crash on our couch."*

We pulled into a parking lot of a laundromat and at first I did not see him and called him. The last time I saw him was a couple of months prior to this when I went to his house he was living at to retrieve some items I left. He was his usual crazy and chaotic self. I did not notice anything off or out of the ordinary, other than he was smoking synthetic weed. He asked me to take him to get more and I did. I always did. This night as I waited in my car on the phone to him, I saw a skeleton of a man stand up and walk towards my car. My jaw dropped as I hung up the phone with his.

"Oh my God!" I exclaimed. My fiancé asked what the matter was. I looked at him and pointed towards the man walking from the laundromat and towards my car. I watched him move in slow motion, methodically moving towards me. "Who is that?' My fiancé asked. "My brother." I sorrowfully answered. His dark set blue eyes were sunken in, he moved with pain but did not show it. His cheekbones were so prominent, they looked like they would cut through his skin and protrude out. His pants hung off of him, he kept pulling them up as he walked, despite wearing a belt. I took a deep breath in and let it out forcibly. "He's using again." I told my fiancé. "How do you know?' he asked. "Do you not see what I see?" I answered as my brother opened the back passenger door and slid into the seat behind my fiancé. I turned and looked at him. He smiled that million-dollar smile of his and immediately went into his, 'what's going on, Rach!' as he shut the door. I just looked at him and half assed smiled. I think he knew what I knew, and he said no more. I turned over the ignition and sat a moment looking out at the laundromat sign. I did not turn to him, I just looked out the windshield and spoke. "You will not bring that shit into my house and around my kids, do you hear me?' I demanded as I turned to look at him in his wide glassy eyes. He just looked at me and nodded his understanding.

We drove home to his incessant chatter of where he had been the last month. He told me of a drug-filled adventure and grand scheme to go to Arkansas and work with a buddy of his, and then decided to head to Nashville to try his hand at singing. He rambled on in an excited, manic, manner that made my already pounding head spin. I should have been used to this by now. He was always on a constant whirlwind between using and sobriety and sometimes they merged together. He was what we addicts call, a functioning addict. He would use it in order to work and work in order to use.

They say marijuana is a gateway drug, but that isn't true. If we peel back the layers of an addict, we more times than not, find trauma. Drugs helped to escape the trauma and abuse I suffered as a child, and I cannot help but think that they did the same for my brother. I look back at old photographs and I used to focus on my own pain. You could clearly see running rampant across my face, and now when I see these old photos, I can see his. Pain he never spoke of trauma he never healed from. Just lost in the euphoria that burned through his veins, so he didn't have to speak or heal from. Sometimes, that is just easier.

Growing up with him was an adventure in itself. He was forever the big brother, forever the protector and sometimes the antagonist. He was your typical big brother to a baby sister. Outwardly never wanting me to tag along, but inwardly glad I did. I found out later, through a slip up from him, he would make sure I was with him and my other brother, so I wouldn't be at the mercy of my abuser. Like I said, forever the protector. He never revealed too much to me, always stopping short of any explanation or details. As I got older, my own repressed memories filled in the blanks. He took a lot of my pain and all of his and held it in so tight that it consumed him in hate and grief. Always wondering why, I would ever help the one that hurt me. His only reprieve was the poison he pumped through his body, a notion I myself personally know.

    I have seen him sober, and I have seen him not, but what I saw that night I picked him up from that run down laundromat, I did not recognize. This was not brother; I have never seen him in such distress and disarray. I have seen and I have witnessed firsthand the devastation drugs can do to a person, to their body, to their demeanor and character. I watched my dad spiral as well as both my brothers, and I watched my own affair with hell slaughter the person I was meant to be.

    He spent a few days surfing my couch and when I say a few, I mean it. It only takes a few days for the pain to set in and the call of the craving screaming in your ears to make you move and seek out the relief it so desperately needs. He came to me one morning, sweating and eating everything in my house, a side effect of not eating or drinking for extended periods of time, wanting to borrow my car. I told him no, but that he could use my fiancé's truck. He swore it was to go do a plumbing job, and I believed him. Or maybe it was what I wanted to believe that is. Every fiber in my person screamed to not let him, tore at my conscience to not do the very thing I did, and gave him the keys to the truck.

The love for an addict is unbearable at most. It is difficult to maintain, it is heartbreaking and detrimental to the whole of things. The love I had, no have, for my brother runs deeper than any other I have encountered. I hold his secrets in my person, forever under lock and key. It was his love for me that overpowered the common sense to show him tough love and say no. I was so blinded by that, that I went against my own sobriety sometimes and caved under the pressure. Afraid that I would lose the very person who fought and saved me so many times, it was only fair that I do the same, right?

Unknowingly so, or perhaps turning a blind eye, not wanting to see the forest for the trees, I once again gave in. The promises he made fell on semi-deaf ears. With addicts the promises become thrown around like glitter, cluttering everything and serving no purpose. We hold onto them thinking maybe this time they mean it. Goes back to love tainting our visions and clouding our judgment. But when is it enough? When do we lift the veil and take off the blinders? When do we take our own lives back and realize this type of love is toxic to you both?

Three days later is when I did. When I got a phone call from a police officer wanting to know if I knew the person who was driving my fiancé's truck. He didn't have a driver's license and he was high. They were going to have to impound the truck and wanted to know if I could come get him. I think I said several hundred explicit words and told the officer he could call someone else because I was not coming to get him, and I hung up the phone. Two days after that, my car dealership called, pissed they had to go get our truck. Two days after that my brother called, I couldn't tell you what he wanted, I didn't care. I had had enough. I was infuriated and I told him so. I told him I never wanted to see him again, to not call me anymore, that I was done with his shit, and I hung up the phone. I blocked him on everything. Yes, I was that mad.

Yes, I caught hell for it too. I did not care, I was done. It had been me to answer the calls, me to go get him all hours of the night, me to write to him and accept phone calls when he was in prison, me to keep his secrets from his wife when he would call me to 'hook him up,' because I knew people. It had been ME and I was done. He would try to reach me any way he could. Hurt, no doubt, that his baby sister shunned him. I stuck to my guns, and I did not talk to him, I did not see him, I did not entertain any aspect of the liking. I did not see I would regret that decision to this day.

It hurt me to tell him these things, it tore at my heart something fierce. But I could not do it anymore, I could not watch him spiral into nothingness, I just could not do it. It was not for lack of love for him, or the want to help him, it was a lack of love for the choices he made in his life that led him to this destruction. I saw him start to decline six months prior and I ignored it, I shouldn't have. I justified it, I rationalized it, I said well 'it's just weed', then it went to,' it's just synthetic weed, it's legal you can get it anywhere.' These are not the justifications or validations that solved anything. I kick myself as I remember a moment standing in his den with him, his son and girlfriend. I was shaking my head at the fact that he was smoking with his 16-year-old son at the time when his son turned blue and was gasping for air. He slapped him on his back, and I rushed over and laid him down. Having to revive my own nephew as his father stood idly by too fucked up to even comprehend what was happening makes my stomach turn this very day. You would think at the moment he realized what the hell just happened that that would prompt him to stop.

I had no idea the 'it's just weed,' was far more than I anticipated. I never thought he would fall back into the harder shit. He vowed to not do anything heavier than weed when his son was born, and for the most part he held onto that partial sobriety. I am not trying to drag my brother and his illness through the mud, I am only offering some context, some sort of understanding into this tale that is anything but that. If not for my own understanding into the why of it. I cannot speak on what transpired in his life the years I was not there, dealing with my own hell, but I am not here to speak on that. I am here to talk about a sister's love for her addict brother, and the moment the cold took over my soul.

A month after the truck incident, I was preparing the final touches on the most wonderful day of my life so far. A day second to the birth of my boys. My wedding day. Even though I had been married previously, this one I wanted. This one I will keep forever. A day and night forever ingrained into my psyche fighting over where to file it under, joy or sorrow. Turns out, it would be both. I was busy with RSVP's and making sure every detail was perfect. I learned my brother was staying with my dad and I called my stepmom to confirm they would be ok to drive as my dad had trouble riding long distances in the car. I heard my brother's voice and asked my stepmom if he was there. Ever the hot-headed stubborn ass I am, she asked me if I wanted to talk to him, and I said no but asked her if she would ask him if he were going to attend the wedding. Yes, I know not very Jesus of me to stoop to high school level bullshit, no excuse, I did, I was petty, angrily so. He confirmed he wouldn't miss it and I left it at that. I continued with my wedding festivities and focused on the task at hand.

December 31, 2015, nationally marked for the end of an era and the precursor to a new, a day of chaos, joy, mishaps and laughs. A day I will forever cherish, not just for the pure excitement of finally being with a man who loved me in all the right places, or the fact that two families joined together made up of blood and oil, but also for the images I chose to hold onto of my brother. I spent the better part of the day running on coffee and adrenaline with my cousin and soon to be bonus daughter doing what I suspect most brides to be do before they take that walk down the aisle, hair, nails, and of course waxing eyebrows and mustaches. I had a private session later for my hair and makeup, but my cousin and bonus daughter needed to shine as well. My cousin was one of my matrons of honor, I had two, and my bonus daughter was just going to look beautiful regardless of the fact she had no role in this shindig. I was nervously excited, and anxiously, worried. Yes worried, I mean what could possibly go wrong right?

Everything thus far was on schedule and according to plan. I had a few kinks to work out, but I was not worried about it. It would get handled or it wouldn't, I was more concerned with getting to the venue and putting myself together for this event of events. The greatest day of my life was about to commence, and I was as ecstatic as I was nervous. I could not shake the heaviness I felt in my stomach, the foreboding naw at my neck. I chalked it up to wedding day jitters and looking back…well hindsight is always 20/20. I sat surrounded by friends and family in a conference room of the venue. Clothes, shoes, hair care products, and make-up strung everywhere. Lighter exploding as everyone talked and carried on, excited to be here with me and sharing this day with me. I have never in my life had so many people turn up for anything I have ever done. Not a graduation, not a baby shower, nothing and I was amazed at the fact that everyone I invited came and then some. The room I was in was packed and I would soon find out so was the rest of the place.

My mom came strutting in as she always had to be the center of attention and the look on her face told me she knew she was not and I should have known then what shit she would cause, but this is not a Debra show tale. Not entirely though. I asked her one thing and that was whether or not my brother was there. You see I have three brothers, two older and one younger. Now I love my younger brother, he is more of a son to me than a brother as he is only two years older than my oldest son, but my older two, they hold a place in my heart I have yet to find a match to. My middle brother was not able to attend my wedding. A fate he himself sealed and was serving the time needed to rectify that mistake, so despite my anger towards my oldest brother, I wanted, no I needed him there. I could not shake for the life of me why the need to see him was so great. I mean what he did, and the anger I felt, why would I care if he showed up to this thing, right?

But something tugged at me something fierce, and it did not subside until I saw his face. I walked down the aisle and scanned it looking for him, I saw pictures later of me looking distraught as I walked hand in hand with my dad to meet the man who would take me from him, and I did not realize the weight was showing as I looked desperately for my brother in the sea of eyes that were on me. The feeling subsided a little as I watched the man of my dreams catch my eye and held me there as I walked up the steps and into his hands. I held his stare as everyone settled into their seats and all my focus was on him and the words of the chaplain. My whole body was shaking and as I repeated the words the Chaplin said to me, tears flowed heavily down my cheeks and smeared the horrendous makeup job, making it almost bearable. That is a story in itself, another time though. I closed my eyes and kissed the man before me as everyone clapped and stood and cheered a new couple into existence. As we walked back down the aisle as man and wife, I once again scanned the crowd for those deep-set blue eyes and that million-dollar smile. I did not voice my concern to anyone, I simply began to let the disappointment of him not showing up to set in. The photographer gathered everyone around and began to take his preplanned photos of the families and friends. He stood me up with my youngest brother at the altar, and as he posed us, I looked up and down the aisle came my disheveled, wide eyed, tucking his shirt into his pants that he probably threw on while in the car, brother. He saw me and flashed that million-dollar smile and practically ran the rest of the way to me. He was lit and it showed in his glassy eyes, but he was there, and that is all that mattered at the time. I wanted to recreate a photo we did at his wedding and so I posed him and my younger brother on either side of me and had the photographer take the picture. One I will covet and not ever give up to anyone.

   Sitting at the wedding party table after the first dances and the food was served, he walked over to me and sat down beside me. I looked at him, still angry but glad he finally showed up. No words were exchanged, he just scooted the chair closer to me, smiled at me and rubbed my back the way someone does for comfort. I smiled back and leaned into his sideways hug, and just like that all was forgiven. Call it divine intervention, call it fate, call it whatever you want, I called it rectified. No one knew the events that would transpire after, no one could have predicted it, but looking at it now, I think I did. I think the nagging, insufferable feeling I had was more than wedding day jitters. I think the excitement of the day tangled in the premonition and clouded its clarity and I simply did not see.

   I recall asking my husband 'Why didn't I tell him to come home with me?' and 'Why did I let him leave?' Answers to which he had none. Looking back, I am not convinced it would have made a bit of good if he had come home with me that night, not convinced that I would have been able to change his fate. I believe in predestination, and I believe we all have an hourglass of life and when it has run out of sand, we can't just flip it over. No matter how much we may want to, we can't interpret, disrupt, or change anyone else's life, path or journey, we are only in control of our own, and honestly, not even then.

    We were set to take a cruise for our honeymoon. An adventure neither of us had ever partook, we were both excited to leave and we were due to set sail in three days. New Year's Eve was quiet in our home, we chose not to attend the after-party festivities of ringing in the new year with our friends and family and decided to just rest at home with our kiddos. We left the clean-up of the establishment to some of the patrons, and we took our leave as husband and wife back to our home. It was already an eventful day and night and others saw to it to make sure we ended with the unveiling of wedding gifts. I half expected my brother to show up with the rest of them at my house, but I was told he was taking my nephew home. He had accompanied his dad to my wedding, and I was happy to have him there with his girlfriend, missing his sister and mom. My brother was divorced from their mom, but she was still family nonetheless, and she continues to be to this day. I was not upset that he did not, I was relieved actually as I already had a houseful and did not want any more than that. After the gifts and the crowd left, the house was quiet. I remember it being eerily quiet. The exhaustion from the day did not allow me to ponder on the fact of a strangely quiet house and I went to bed next to my new amazing husband.

    I was plagued with dreams, and I tossed and turned all night. Unable to make sense of the dream, I have tried so many times to do so, but it was gibberish at best. Fluttering images of my childhood mixed with events of my life, and images of my brothers in places I did not recognize. I woke earlier than normal and grudgingly got up to a sickening feeling in the pit of my stomach. Again, unsure as to what it was, I simply tried to shrug it off and I went about my day with preparing for our cruise. My husband had to work that night, and as I spent the day doing housework, I was folding laundry on the couch with my middle son watching T.V, mainly for background noise. The phone rang.

   My mom came on the line and asked me if I had heard from my brother that day. I told her not since the night before at the wedding. She asked if I would call him as he was not answering her calls. Little side note, he rarely answered her calls if ever. She expressed to me that there was a rumor going around that he was injured, and I remember telling her,*' Mom, do you hear yourself, a rumor? Come on now, he is probably high somewhere, but I'll call.'* So, I did and did not get any answer as well, I left a voicemail, and I sent a text. I called my mom back and let her know that I did not get an answer either but that I left a voicemail and text and would let her know if he responds. She replied with,*' well your aunt called and told me he was dead. Can you call your cop friend and ask if he would run his name?'*

   Annoyed, I said I would, and I called him to ask if he would run his name, he said he would and would call me back. I no sooner hung up with him when

my mom called again telling me that I needed to go to this address and tell the paramedics he was my brother. Confused as to what she was telling me, I asked several times *'what do you mean?'*
I will never forget these next words, ever. She answered,*' I don't know what happened, all I know is Summer called her mom to ask her what she should do, and she told her to call 911. They have been working on your brother for 30 mins now and need someone to go identify him.'*

    The guttural scream that escaped my body woke the dead. My son who was sitting next me jumped up as I threw my phone and went tail spinning into the kitchen, and he caught me as I went down and carefully placed me on the floor. Everything after that went black and I became robotic, unbelieving of what I just heard. My son took the address down that my mom tried to give, and he walked over to where I was still sitting on the floor and yelled at me to get up and go. I remember looking up at him and taking the paper and my phone from him. My mom was still on the line, I did not speak to her again. I hung it up and began calling my husband at work, as he had the only vehicle we had at the time. It was already dark, about 8 or 9 I cannot tell you which. The concept of time simply vanished from my mind. Still trying to call my husband I rushed over to the neighbors and asked them if they would take me to get the truck from him. I gave them a brief rundown of the situation and they quickly rushed me over to his work. At his work I angrily yelled for him to give me the keys as my mom called his phone to tell him to not let me drive. Yea that didn't work, nice try though. I took his keys as my aunt called telling me not to come that she was already headed that way. For the first time ever, I cussed at her. I told her. *'Fucked that, he is MY brother, I am on my way."*

   That drive was the longest drive I have ever taken, no traffic, late at night, and speeding, still felt like an eternity to drive 15 miles. The whole way there I just kept repeating over and over again, *not my brother, not my brother, please God not my brother.* Not even paying attention to the road, oblivious to any cars on the road. It is a wonder I did not wreck; it is a miracle I did not get stopped for going 90 miles an hour. I later found out that my amazing cop friend cleared a path for me, told me he radioed my truck in and the situation. He even assigned himself to work the scene even though it was not his area to patrol.

   I caressed a curve and slid to a halt behind three cop cars, blue lights lit the desolate area, illuminating the street in flickering chaos. I jumped out of the truck, I did not even shut the door, I don't even know how it got shut or who did it. I started running the minute my feet hit the pavement. My aunt and uncle, already there, as well as my cop friend. I ran, I managed to dodge my aunt and uncle as they tried to stop me. Only to be almost clothes lined by my cop friend and one other policeman standing there with him. I crashed into them; my friend held me there a minute as I fought against his hold. My aunt came up to us and he sort of shoved me into her. She held on to me as she told me," Rachael, *it's him, he's gone."* And I went down screaming, she held on to me as we both went down. My uncle hoovered over both of us.

I started screaming at my friend to let me see him, he tried so gingerly to calm me down, but I wasn't having it. I screamed at him that I needed to see for myself it was him. He took a deep breath and yelled,*' I AM NOT LETTING YOU DO ANY DAMN THING UNTIL YOU CALM THE HELL DOWN!'* I went silent, he asked me once more if I was going to stay calm and I nodded as he helped me up and walked to the door of the house where my brother laid dead. He stood in the doorway and told me that I could not go any further than that. He had to get permission for me to even go that far.

He held out his hand and told me it would be alright and led me into the house. The first thing I saw was a small TV leaning against the wall that faced the door and the smell of asphalt hit my nose. Drug houses have a distinct smell to them. The stench seeps into the floors and the walls and no amount of cleaning will ever get the smell out. But this house had the familiar smell of melted asphalt and pennies. I did not want to look away from the TV or the wall, I remember thinking how odd it was for a TV to be plugged in and leaning against the wall facing the door. It was just a weird scene. He assured again that it would be ok and held out his hand and placed it on my shoulder in an awkward show of comfort. He said, *'look Rachael, is that your brother?'* There lying prone in the middle of the floor, a bulb bag tube sticking out of his mouth, naked aside from a small cloth covering his groin, laid my brother. I told my friend that it was indeed my brother and as if he knew what I was about to ask, he said, *'No Rachael you can't go over there."* He led me out of the house, back into the blue lights of the night. My aunt was standing in the same spot I left her in, she watched me with tear-soaked eyes as I came solemnly down the stairs and stood in front of her. No words were needed, for she saw what I saw, and she was feeling what I was feeling. She just hugged me, held me there for a moment and then asked if I wanted to sit in her car to warm up.

My aunt and I have a bond like no other, one forged from trauma and sealed in love and that January night, it became forged in an unforgettable, infallible, fire. One that has strengthened what we already had, one that we share separately but hold equally. One where, when I look at her, I no longer see my aunt, no, I see myself standing in the cold of a blue light night.

I cannot tell when my parents showed up, all I can tell you is my mom was there before my dad. We all stood outside that house waiting for the medical examiner to come and get my brother. My friend would not let anyone in the house as it was an active crime scene. He did tell me however some of the events that went down that tragic night. My baby cousin was the one to call 911, but that I feel is the only good thing she did this night. According to police recollections, I say recollections, because the police report told a completely different story; My cousin and her boyfriend for lack of a better term, were in the house with other drug users, who I cannot say. They scattered like roaches in the light when the cops showed up. According to my cousin, she said she shot my brother up, but did not use any of what she gave my brother herself, even though she had been before this incident. She said that afterwards my brother complained of indigestion and was going to go take a shower and lay down. She said he went to the bathroom, heard him turn on the shower and then heard him yell out. She went to check on him and found him on the floor of the bathroom. She said she panicked and called her mom, who instructed her to call 911. In which she did. The amount of time she talked to her mom, I cannot tell you, there are conflicting stories, but I do know her mom kept telling her to get off the phone with her and call 911.

According to the police, when they showed up my cousin was cleaning up the house frantically and they found my brother on the floor of the living room. The fact that she was cleaning and did not run with the others in the house threw everyone for a loop, so much so that the cops detained her, put her in handcuffs and placed her in the back of a squad car. I was told that they were looking for anything to arrest her as her story kept changing as the events of the night. The true, true story lies with my cousin and my brother and well two can keep a secret if one of them is dead. There is room to believe she gave him a hotshot, but again only she can say what actually happened that night.

  Confused by this, I could not bring myself to walk over to the cop car and talk to her through the partially rolled down window. My family members tried but she just kept saying she didn't know what happened. When the medical examiner finally showed up the cold had set up residence in my soul and I am still unsure if I were numb from the below freezing temperatures, the pain, or both. I learned that they could not move my brother's body until the medical examiner got there as she is the authority in these situations. She is the one to say the manner of death and whether or not foul play may or may not have occurred.

  My mother had already arranged for the funeral home to come get my brother, but she did not have the authority nor the right to do so. She was quickly told that even the funeral home has to wait on the M.E. My mother would put on an extravagant show of bullshit from this point on. The police secured the house and closed the door once the medical examiner was on the scene. They had already been keeping people out of the house, but the door had been opened partially up to this point. I stood in the middle of the yard watching the house, unaware of the cold, of the people around me. My mom had offered me a blanket and I declined it. I did not want to be touched, bothered, nothing. This notion offended her, and she threw the blanket in my face, prompting my Granny to scold her daughter.

I heard a commotion behind me, and I turned to see what was going on, and I saw my dad walking up the road and I bolted, nearly knocking him down as I slammed into him sobbing, *'he's dead daddy, he's dead!"* He held onto me as we both walked back to the yard, my mom started screaming at him, unsure as to why. Her oldest sister and nephew grabbed her and held onto her as she hysterically sobbed. I have no doubt she was in pain, none. Losing a child is one of the hardest things a mother can go through, I myself have buried one, however, you will soon realize my angst. My dad let go of me and went to my mom, my brother after all was their oldest. She let him console her for a hot second before my stepmom came over and she literally pushed my dad backwards with enough force he stumbled.

I went over to where my cop friend was standing and I asked him if he could make sure that my parents did not see my brother that way, to ask if the M.E would cover him. He did that very thing, and they wheeled my brother out in a black body bag that was lit up with the blue lights of the night. My mom asked the M.E if she could see him and she promptly told her NO. This infuriated my mom and she yelled, 'BUT I"M HIS MOTHER!' This did not sway the M.E or her techs as they put my brother in the back of her van. My mom tried to get some information out of the M.E as she closed the back door of the van and maneuvered around the crowd of people surrounding it. My mom told her that the funeral home was in transit and was quickly told that they can turn around until after the autopsy. The M.E had enough suspicion and evidence that this was more than an accidental overdose.

Here is where I will say this, the events of that night are scattered as there were multiple people there and each of them have their version of that frigid night, and this is mine. I do not care who it upsets, I do not care who this offends, I do care that my brother died in vain, he suffered in life. Plagued with demons of his own making and ones he tried to conquer. He took every hurt, every pain, every triumph, every burn in his veins, everything he tried to keep me safe from, to his grave. The events of that night were nothing but suspect and deemed a further investigation and when it was all said and done, he was just another junkie.

When the M.E took my brother away we were able to go into the house and only retrieve belongings of my brother's that were in plain sight. If we could not see it, we could not take it. My mom and I were allowed to go with the accompaniment of my dear friend. The first thing I noticed when I re-entered that dreadful home was a blood stain where my brother was laying. Not where you might expect a bloodstain to be. It was in the place where his back was, high up by his shoulder blades. The image of my brother lying there will haunt me for all my days, so the bloodstain was not where it should be. If he had a heart attack, like they thought he had, why was blood there in that particular spot. I moved from the living room down a hallway looking at the floor. The floor was dry, free from any evidence of moving a wet, apparently bloodied body from the bathroom to the living room, and why was he in the living room if he fell in the bathroom? The hallway was wide enough for paramedics.

   In a back bedroom I found my brother's clothes strewn around on a bed, his wallet laid on the floor next to his phone. My brother would not have walked butt naked from bedroom to the bathroom, he was notorious for leaving his wallet in his pants along with his phone. Wallet empty aside from his driver's license. We gathered his things there in that room. A small milk crate held his work boots and some tools, my mom tried to go through drawers but was quickly told she could on get what she could see. We both walked out of the room and into the bathroom. Into a pristine bathroom, free of any water, debris or splatter. The shower looked as if no water had ever graced its tub or curtain, no water on the floor, no wet towels, nothing. I have never seen a cleaner bathroom, especially in a known drug house.

   That is when I remembered my cousin was cleaning the house when the paramedics showed up and I told my mom that very thing when she commented on the bone-dry bathtub, a detail she did not know up to that point. As we walked back out of the house, my mom was on a mission to have the head of her formal baby niece. My cousin was the daughter of my dad's baby sister. My mom wanted her to be charged and was infuriated at the fact that she was not being charged. She went on to yell obscenities and say things like, *'she had a hit out on him.'* Now I do not know if this statement is 100% accurate. All I have to go on is the story my brother told of an incident where he was attacked by a guy, we all thought was his friend. He rambled on about it being a set up, and well no one has ever confirmed or denied this accusation. Is it possible, sure, anything is possible?   Now I know I just painted a very gruesome picture and well it was quite raw in nature and that is just how I tell a story, honest, raw, somewhat offensive, but I always come back around with something good.

    My brother was more than his addiction. He was an amazing big brother growing up. Almost like a father figure. He did not allow anyone to mistreat, disrespect, hurt or harm me or my middle brother. Sure, there were fights all siblings fight and argue, but we three were and still are very close despite the turbulent childhood we had. My brothers were star athletes. I loved to watch them both play football and have attended every single game they ever played. Michael, I know I have not mentioned his name before it is hard to even say it, was phenomenal, a football prodigy, I had no doubt he would have gone pro had the devil not got a hold of him.

He was charismatic and could charm the pants off anyone. He had a million-dollar smile that got him into just as much trouble as it did out of trouble. Intelligent beyond means, he was once suspended from school for fighting for a month, came back and aced a Trigonometry test without even being prepared for it. He was funny and loved to laugh but had a fire in him you didn't ever want to see. He did not want kids, true story, he was afraid he would treat them how we were treated growing up and he couldn't see doing that to anyone else. However, he was an amazing father, despite being smoking buddies with his teenage son. He adored that boy and even more so his daughter. He often would say he saw his sister in his daughter when she would pick on her older brother. This always got a laugh out of me and a "that's my girl!' My boys were adored by him as well, he would light up every time they were in his presence and they returned the adoration.

Addiction just does not destroy the body, but it infects and infests everything in its wake. It destroys all that was once an amazing person and turns it all black and leaves it to rot. The loved ones hold on to the person that is underneath it all. Hoping and praying that one day they will make it to the other side of it all and have one hell of a story to tell. The unfortunate truth of it all, the ones that do are a rare breed. I am only typing this as a reminder that I was one that made it out alive. What I have left of my brother are the memories and every now and again I see him in my now oldest brother, my boys, and myself when the light hits me just right in the mirror.

    The night of his death, it shook me so violently that I spun out of control and six months would go by before I even started to recover from it. When everyone left the scene, I was the last to go. Gently being coaxed by my cop friend to leave. I sat on the porch of that death house, and I was lost in the blue lights dancing against the early morning night. I was numb from inside out, just lost in the whole world. I do not remember being walked to my car or getting in or driving home. The house was eerily quiet when I returned, every soul asleep or at least in their rooms, I could not tell you if they were asleep or not, my guess is, no. My husband laid awake in the bed and did not say a word to me as I laid down next to him. He covered me up and held me gently. I did not realize that I was almost hypothermic being in the cold unprotected. I left the house the night before in flip flops, a sweatshirt and leggings in the brittle Oklahoma January cold. I was oblivious to it, my mind shut down every receptor to any physicality of my being. I could not discern cold from numb or numb from heartbreak.

    It was not until I started to shiver under the warmth of the blankets that I realized my core was frozen, my husband, being the ever-ready soldier, stripped his clothes off and mine and laid skin to skin with me until the shivering stopped. He never said a word, just held me close and rocked me gently. I must have fallen asleep out of sheer exhaustion because a vivid dream woke me two days later. I still remember it to this day six years later. *I am on a road trip, destination unknown, in a car with my middle brother and we come to this drawbridge. It was down and we began to cross as the waters rose quickly around us. The bridge started to rise and so did the water. It surrounded our car, and we began to shift against the raging current. Jeremy, my middle brother, jumps out of the car and onto the hood of it. He holds out his hands and yells, 'Stop and be still!' The water stops and plummets back into the ocean and recedes back to a calm flow of waves against the shore as we start to move across the bridge. Jeremy crawls back into the car and tells me, "It will be ok sis, I got you!"*

      It was so vivid and clear, it jolted me awake. I woke to a bright sun beaming through the window and on my face. I remember blinking against it as the light engulfed me, I laid there replaying the night before in my head. I later learned I had slept for two days straight. Every chance to rouse me was futile. I did not eat, but there were cups on the bedside table so I suppose I did drink, though I cannot recall. There isn't much I recall in those six months I was lost wandering into the abyss, except darkness and confusion. The cold still sitting heavy in my gut, the blue light night stuck on repeat running savagely through my brain. I remember the look everyone gave me as I emerged from my hole, the look of surprise and pity but mainly of loss. Loss of words to say or of any comfort they may try to offer. They walked on eggshells around me, unsure as to what to do or say.

My oldest asked if I were O.K and I simply nodded and walked over to the fridge. I remember standing in front of it holding the door open and being swallowed by the yellow light that glowed from it. Looking for something and nothing at the same time. Everyone still watching me as I closed the fridge and went back to bed. My husband walked into the room and stood there watching me. He asked if I was hungry, I said no. He stood there awhile; I could feel his stare on me as I watched the ceiling. I rolled over and went back to sleep. Images of my brother fluttered behind my eyelids, I would continue to have dreams of him talking to me, visiting me. Dreams not of the past, but as if he were still here. Dreams I came to cherish and would mourn when the morning came.

I did not attend his funeral; I was outright furious at the spectacle my mom made of my brother. She did deplorable things that I have only just begun to forgive her for. The decision I made to not attend his funeral I would be lying if I said it was a bad one, but it was not. It was a decision I made to honor the brother I knew, not the one that was being paraded around to suit the needs of an incredulous person. I do not hate my mother, no, I feel sorry for her. I was stricken with grief and anger, and it fueled animosity and the outrageous charade she put on during this time of horrendous anguish, I have deemed grievous at best. I have no doubt she was hurting, but I also know the performances she puts on to have the attention focused on her. This is not a tale to bash my mom, no, it is simply a sad truth in the thick of it.

    The death of my brother affected us all tremendously and I personally know what it is like to bury a child, so looking back at my anger at the situation, I find myself ashamed. Ashamed of how my grief treated people. Ashamed of how I cursed everyone around me when all I wanted was understanding and comfort. Ashamed at the words I spoke to undeserving people, ashamed that I lost one of the only people who loved me unconditionally, and I pushed him away like garbage. I was angrier with myself than I was with anyone or anything else. I came to believe that the last night I saw him, the universe knew it would be my last. I think I kind of knew it too. The churning in my gut, the anxious wait for him to show up, I have never cared whether he showed or not, but that night I did.

    I tried to go back to some form of normality. Some form of busy and preoccupation so I did not have to deal with the emotions that were wreaking havoc on my soul. I became angrier by the day. The tailspin had started, and I found myself struggling to stay above it. So, I do what every rational, grief-stricken person does, I go back to work. I learned quickly that it was a mistake. Three weeks went by, and I was robotic at best. When I was not working, I would go from the bed to the couch to the fridge. A devastating cycle that plummeted me further into the abyss. Unaware still of my surroundings, going through motions of muscular memory and a facade of the *'I'm ok'*. The anger boiling inside me, but the cold still sat solid in my gut, sizzling but never melting. Never leaving my soul, forever letting me feel the emptiness it released fueling the beast that emerged outwardly.

I was so blinded by grief that I didn't even realize it was seeping over onto my family and my life. So consumed by anger and rage, I was unwittingly burning those close to me. I stopped being a wife to my husband, only going through the motions of it. Stopped taking care of myself, stopped being a mom and became a shell of the person they knew and loved. I was mean to everyone. Nasty even. No amount of apologies can ever make up for the damage my grief did. Most tragically of all, I was all those things to myself. I laid down and allowed grief to take control and allowed anger and rage to be co-pilots. I have a journal that I wrote in during this time and it is completely filled. I am terrified to read it now, to see the proof of the devastation that the death of my brother created. I know if I ever want to completely heal from it, I have to swallow that fear and read it. I let it all transform me into a wrath filled monster that does not, to this day, deserve the love my boys, my husband, my family gave to me tenfold during this time. I honestly can't tell you where I would be now if it weren't for their love helping me through it all.

I had a glimmer of hope when I learned my other brother was being released from prison, but it was soon extinguished when the realization of the fact he did not get to say goodbye to his brother, nor had he seen him the entire time he was incarcerated. This set a new precedence of grief and another layer to the cold in my gut. My heart broke all over again. I hurt more for him than I did for myself, or perhaps my hurt was just amplified by his. Either way, the tailspin continued to shove me deeper into this black hole of mourning.

I lost time, I couldn't remember if I showered one day from the next. My husband picked up the pieces and suffered greatly for it. I either didn't eat or I ate everything sometimes to the point of vomiting. I wore the same pajamas; I rarely did laundry or cleaned the house. I cooked out of obligation but did not eat with them, I did wifely duties for the same reason. I was nothing, I was walking, talking, oblivion. I took the shattered pieces of my heart and soul, and I shoved into a junk drawer, tighten the straps of my body armor and gave Anger the reins. Completely lost control of it all yet held it together so eloquently.

I wanted to escape it all, I did not want to feel this pain I was in. The euphoria after the burn never came, it burned and writhed in my veins like lava. Searing the very essence of my person. So the path of self-destruction was paved and I rode down it like a surfer on a kahuna of a wave. I did what I knew to, what I had learned to do. I survived by any means necessary. Telling myself over and over that I was *'ok, he was in a better place, and we all should be grateful.'* So, I ran. I ran from the acceptance, from the help I needed, from the family I created, I ran from myself. Searching for the anecdote. Oblivious to the fact that it laid within me. That I had the ingredients to make it.

    I ran, literally, to another state. Looking for solace and reprieve, looking for anything other than the current situation I was in. I was not only hurting from my brother's death, but there were issues my husband bequeathed to me when we married that I could no longer deal with, so I ran. Fully believing that it was not running or retreating but removing myself from it all. Removing myself from the physical would remove the metaphysical, right? Oh, how wrong I was. I was so naive to consider the notion that just because you put space and opportunity between it all, doesn't not mean it is removed, or healed, or even dealt with. But I did not care. I ran, no I fled two states away, 749 miles to be exact.

    Alone and determined to not have any more shit in my life, my house, anywhere. I left my kids, my husband, and my dogs. They soon followed, but for the first time in a long time I felt as if I could breathe. And I suppose I did for a brief moment, another glimmer of hope that 'healing' was on the horizon. It was not long before the cold awakened and gut punched me so viciously that I am still catching my breath to this day. May 14, 2018, two years, four months and fourteen days after the death of my brother, I received another bone chilling phone call from my mom telling me my nephew overdosed. Michael's beloved boy, not even 18 years old at the time, his mother came home from work that Mother's Day morning and found her son unresponsive in his bed. I know the pain of losing a child and a sibling, and my niece and sister-in-law now share that pain. Not a fate anyone should ever brag about sharing. I will forever hold her and my niece so close to my heart even more so than I ever had.

What was left of my heart, shattered. I was at a job interview and the floor fell out from under me and I collapsed on the floor. Collecting myself I rushed out of that office and dialed my sister in law's number and begged her to tell me it was not true. Tears consumed my eyes, and it is a wonder I made the 35 miles home. Unable to drive the 749 miles back to Oklahoma, I was devastated and alone. I just sat on the couch at my best friend's house in utter shock and dismay. Luck be a son of a bitch for sure. Although you can't really group luck and death in the same basket, but damn, it sure felt like if it weren't for bad luck, we wouldn't have any. I suppose in hindsight I chose luck as an alternative to anything else. Hell, I felt I had exhausted all the others at play at this point so why not? Selfish to even think this tragedy happened to only me. No, not entirely so, we all were still hurting, still grieving the loss of my brother and you throw the loss of his son in the mix of it, it just made the wound fester and bleed even more. My heart absolutely shattered for my niece, she lost more than I or anyone else could ever lose. I can't imagine if I were to have lost my dad around the same time as my brother.

    The tailspin that had slowed ramped up again and Anger awoke Rage and we set off on an adventure of chaos and destruction. Destroying everything in its path. Leaving the rubbage to be picked up by the ones closest to me. My marriage suffered the most. The demands of his time, the constant fights about my rejection of him, the war that raged between my heart and my mind blew carnage all over the life we tried to have together. It was to a point of annihilation. So much so I contacted a divorce attorney and started making plans to leave him, to run again. Countless conversations that turned into arguments and sleepless nights. Me unable, no afraid to confront the monster of grief and despair, lashing out at his incessant clinginess and his own destructive patterns of behavior. A constant struggle of tug of a war with what I was feeling and going through and the demands of a 'good wife'.

Him not understanding what the hell was going on, thinking it was solely him and the stress he added to the situation. In part, he did not help the issue at hand, he compounded it, but it took me breaking completely for him to see through my eyes his part in the matter. It would years later that he finally understood, or began to understand, the devastation of it all. It was his love that helped to pull me back from the abyss, although I am just now able to admit that.

I struggled to maintain work, home, finances, everything. I was barely treading water and the effects of it all were beginning to show on the outside. My armor was leaking, and people were beginning to see through my facade of shit and was being called out on it. I couldn't have that. I couldn't have them coming between myself and my pain. No, it was the only thing I could feel, and I needed it, I craved it, I took it to bed and created my own beautiful paradise of hell. It was mine and no one or nothing was going to take that away from me. I felt that everything else had been ripped from me, and I would be damned if they took my pain too. How dare anyone try and help me heal, who were they to tell me anything they had no idea what I was going through much less how to help me. Right?

I think grief is the ultimate annihilator. I think once she sinks her claws into your veins, her poison slowly rolls through your veins an inch at time. Letting the burn become a part of you, slowly taking over your whole being until it is no longer blood and water in your veins. No longer you in the mirror, no longer your words, your actions, your thoughts. She gives birth to the deepest depression and the duo annihilates the very essence of you. It is a natural process, death. It is a common fate in us all, connecting us if only by that very fact.

With death comes the grief of our loved ones who were left here to endure the process of life without you. Faring better when it was *'our time'* to go versus when they felt *'we were taken too soon.'* But is there a distinction between the two? I believe there isn't. I do not believe there is ever a right time to die, and I believe we must all be ready for it no matter the time of it. That is unpredictable. Unreasonable to even consider we could predict it. I believe grief is a selfish emotion. One birthed from jealousy. I know I felt jealous of my brother dying. I thought, *'how could he leave me here alone and why did he get to rest now?'* I was jealous that I was left here to deal with not only my demons but his. Envious that he now is free from any more pain this world could bestow upon him. Angry at the fact I was jealous of his death. Heartbroken I could never see his face again, jealous of the belief he can still see mine.

I was vengeful, murderess even, if only in thought. I was a tornado wrapped in a hurricane and I did not care who or what I destroyed in my path. I wanted people to feel how I felt, to see and fully understand what I did. I wanted that so much that it blinded me to the chaos, pain, and destruction I was not only doing to myself, but to everyone else as well. My temper became explosive and very short fused. I demanded everything, never asking for forgiveness or offering an apology for my actions. Never cleaning up my own carnage. Forcing everyone else to eat the shit I dealt out as well as their own. I simply lost my ever-loving mind.

So I ran again. This time to the furthest part of the map I could get, 1,236 miles to be exact. I applied to a job, I got an interview, I boarded a plane and flew solo to a place I absolutely knew nothing about to stay with someone I barely knew. Little did I know at that time, that was the best thing I could have done to heal. Up to this point, certain people could not even so much as utter my brother's name. I would shut it down real quick. I felt that certain people didn't have the right to. Their voices seemed to taint it. I would cringe at the sound his name would make when it would escape their lips. It sent shivers down my spine like nails on a chalkboard. Leaving a bitter, metallic taste in my mouth, putrid even. To this day, I have a hard time understanding why. Maybe I will never know, but what I do know is that the number of certain people has significantly dwindled recently.

I would turn the radio off if certain songs triggered the pain. I stopped discussing the fact my brother died, I stopped responding to questions and inquiries. I kept it short and sweet, and I called it healing. I called it 'better than I was'. For all intents and purposes, maybe I was better than I was. I certainly wore a beautiful mask. I was exceptionally good at covering the scars and wounds. Proficient in the smiling face charade that portrayed a 'better Rachael'. However, those that knew me best called bullshit. It would take me another year for me to call out my own bullshit.

JOURNAL ENTRY   26 JAN 2016

' Taking time out seems impossible lately. I can't sit still, I feel like I am tweaking soberly. If I get still my mind wanders, crazy thoughts creep in, I see, I see him. I tear up when I am at work, that will not fly. I don't like questions because the ones asking usually don't have genuine or good intentions of help. I hate to cry, I don't like the feeling of hurting or weakness, BIG GIRLS DON'T CRY. I hate the red eyes and runny nose. The embarrassment of people seeing me like that and the "are you okays?' Busy, stay busy, there's no room for thoughts that make you cry when you're busy.'

2

    Maine is by far one of the most beautiful places you can ever see in the United States. I have yet to experience all the beauty of the States, but Maine is breathtaking. From her rolling hills, extravagant mountains, magnificent sunrises and sunsets, colors fit for a painter's wheel when the leaves begin to change and the picturesque snow that covers everything. To her beautiful beaches and calming waters. I have never seen something so tranquil or magnificent. The vast beauty of her definitely helped to set a broken soul at ease. I was in absolutely amazement at her beauty, but mostly at her quiet solitude and whispering trees. The wind howling through them is something out of a horror movie, and I found it eerily comforting. I found the winds to be cleansing and therapeutic. The howls taking my pain and grief and carrying them away. The midnight black skies in the winter, lit by the moon and stars that cast a blue haze over the night.

    I totally saw firsthand the hypnotic pull Maine had on people and I felt her immensely. The first I felt the icy brick in my gut start to sweat, I was sitting in my car one dark, early morning, about to head to work. The ground was completely covered in snow and the trees bent with the weight of it. I remember thinking, *'man that tiny tree is going to break right in two from all the snow and wind.'* I just knew that if the weather kept up the way it was going it would surely be broken and laying in the yard when I returned home. I sat there a moment longer just watching it bend and creak as clumps of snow fell to the ground and more snow replaced it. Bearing all this weight and never succumbing to it. I watched it in the blue light of the moon and began to cry, unsure as to why, but I did.

   I quickly wiped my face, put my car into reverse and slowly treaded to work on the snow-covered roads. I had an hour and half ride to work and with the current conditions I had to drive slower, watching the road disappear under a cushiony, white, blanket of Maine snow. Listening as it crunched under the weight of my car. The road I stayed on was rarely, if ever, plowed. Or at least plowed last. So the two mile trek out of a valley in snow was challenging at best. Found myself in the ditch a time or two, we won't talk about that. Watching the snowfall was hypnotic in itself, good get lost in the flakes and taken away to faraway places. Reminded me of the intro to The Twilight Zone, youngins' look it up. That particular morning the air was thick with humidity and the snow fell in graceful almost angelic like waves. Once out of the valley the roads were clearer from the plow, and I relaxed a bit and eased my grip on the steering wheel. I had not realized I was squeezing it so tight until I relaxed, and my knuckles cracked from the pressure.

Still leery of the road conditions, but confident enough of the plowing, I settled in for my road trip to work. I often joke about having to pack a lunch to go to Wal-Mart in Maine and well it really wasn't a joke. Maine is notorious for its beauty and infamous for its ruralness. The snow continued to fall, and I drifted back to the tree. The tall, thin tree and the weight it was carrying, and I began to cry again. This time I couldn't stop. I cried the entire way to work. I was dumbfounded as to why I had suddenly become a blubbering idiot on my way to work. Over a tree. Looking at it now, it wasn't the tree, it was me and all the weight I was carrying, bending and creaking against it, getting some reprieve when snow would fall off only to have fresh piled on. At that time, I did not know, or perhaps I didn't want to know why.

My health started to fail prior to my adventure to Maine, and in Maine it all but tanked and after seeing countless doctors, I made a decision that I needed to start taking care of myself better and that needed to start with my mental health. Crying over a tree was, in my book, an indication I was spent mentally and emotionally. We all know how stress can take its toll on a person, add grief and physical ailment to the pot, and well, you have yourself a shit stew of a life. Doesn't sit well with the pallet and I have yet to find a wine that would complement it.

I was attending church at my in-law's church, my father in-law the local pastor there. At first it was nice to get to hear his sermons and see into his life as a pastor. I grew up in the church, literally. My maternal grandfather was a preacher as well as my paternal grandmother. I never felt right sitting in pews, never understanding why. Never comprehending the semantics of it but enjoyed the camaraderie and the community of it. So sitting in a pew next to my mother in-law, felt nice. However, sitting there would be the most I would ever do. I tried to get involved in it, I tried to become this *'good Christian daughter in-law'*, but soon felt the weight of obligation and I did not want that, I needed something else. I needed to heal, and I was not getting that in those pews.

I absolutely love my in-laws. I do not know any other woman that can honestly say she adores her mother-in-law, but I do. I don't have to agree with them in order to love them. I felt I could talk to her; felt she listened and did not judge. She did help me to shed some light on why I was so angry, on why I was so sick, despite God being shoved down my throat, she helped me see past that and let me make up my own mind. That is why I love her so. My husband has told me they were raised the same way. To make up their own minds on the direction of their faith. Odd commodity to me, as I grew up way different than that. I grew up being told that unless I turned it all over to God, got in bed with God, did everything according to God, God, God, then my life would always be crap. That I would never heal, and all my problems were because I turned away from God. Who ever said I did?

 I would come to choke on the very word. Hated it being forced fed. I am a believer in a higher power. I do know that there is something or someone out there that is bigger than I could ever be, greater, wiser. I also believe that it is my free will to believe that I am also my own maker. Without the two coming together, one will not work without the other. Sitting in the pews with my mother-in-law, I was reminded of the suffocating feeling of being force fed religion. I realized that I felt better in nature. I have always loved being outside. Barefoot in the grass feeling the Earth's vibrations seep in through the soles of my feet. Invigorating my soul, constantly reminded that we came from her and we will return to her. And for all you God fearing people, what better way to serve and honor him than being in the midst of all that he created.

 I found that sitting alone in the early mornings, drinking coffee, listening to their clock tick, tears would flow and my mind would drift back to that January night, and I would watch as tears dripped into my coffee. Each tear drop shedding the weight I had been carrying of that night. Not understanding at that moment, that it was not just the grief that would leak through my eyes, but trauma, pain, loss, abuse, all of the weight would release through tears. Each one a snowflake, different from the last.

Writing has always been a way that I could just dump my brain so I could regroup and refocus. So I started doing that very thing. On the mornings of my tear coffee creamer, I would take my phone, open the notes section of it and just type. Before I knew it I had several pages filled and cold cups of coffee. I slowly felt that ice brick in my gut start to melt. I have been alone most of my life, but I have never sat alone with my only company being myself. To sit with yourself, really get into your brain and walk around in it, is not for the faint of heart. The strongest warriors are brought to their knees at the confrontation of themselves. So writing, although easy to do, was rather difficult, brutal, and messy.

I wrote not with the intention of dealing with anything, but so that I could clear my brain of clutter, adjust my armor and tread on. I was ignorantly unaware of the benefit it was bestowing on me. The loss of my brother was embedded deep, intertwined with my soul. Writing seemed to help loosen its grip. The longer I would sit with myself, the tighter the grip, the more I wrote while sitting with myself, the looser it became. It was excruciating, and I found myself struggling to breathe even more so. The constant fluctuation between pain and comfort deeply bruised my intentions. I wanted to stop, I didn't want to hurt anymore as I had become so immune to the pain and grief that the release, no matter how minute, stung and ached something fierce. I didn't know then that the hurt I was feeling, I needed it. The offensiveness of it was justifiable brutality.

My husband suggested that we take up hiking in the backwoods of Maine. A venture that I excitedly welcomed. One spring day when we thought the snow had melted enough, we packed a backpack, donned our hiking boots and headed out to see where the forest would take us. It wasn't long before we were ankle deep in snow, but we didn't care. We trekked on until the only sounds we could hear aside from our breathing was the forest. I stopped and closed my eyes and listened to the voices of the trees, the whispers of the wind, and in my tranquility, I heard my brother's voice. I heard him say, *'listen.'* and I did just that, I listened. Desperate to hear him again, I listened.

I listened to the ice brick in my gut melt some more, I listened to the wind caress my pain and strip it away with each stroke. I listened to the forest as she wrapped her arms around me and held me tight, whispering to me to let it all go. The stubbornness of that which is me, shook out of her grasp and moved fervently through the forest next to my husband, only reveling in her beauty and ignoring her healing. Unwillingly, I emerged from the hike feeling refreshed and more energized, but I justified it as the exercise we obtained from the hike.

We would seek out trails and mountains and beaches to hike. Each time I would feel better and better, but again exercise, right? I have no doubt the exercise helps in recovery, healing, and transformations. I just was not able to discern between those notions at the time. What was healing? What were transformations? What was anything other than the suffering I had known for so long? I was convinced that this was just how it was going to be, and if I could get healthier then that was enough. That was going to be the magic that it took to be free of pain.

My favorite place to be is the beach. I was 34 years old the very first time I saw the ocean. My husband took me to Mississippi the March after our wedding for a late honeymoon and I fell in love with her right then and there. Lost in the cadence of her waves and the soothing voice as they crashed to shore. The smell of salt invigorating my senses. So it only made sense that we seek her out anyway we could. Maine has some of the most beautiful beaches, even those that are rocky, and some of the clearest fresh waters I have ever seen. Reflective even in cloudy skies. Just breathtakingly beautiful. The rivers and lakes are vibrant and alive, the ocean very vocal and calm at the same time. It is no wonder people flock to Maine in the summer months.

I found quiet and solitude on any of her banks, my favorite being the little coves my husband and I would seek out. No tourists, barely even locals, just us and the water. We found a little cove one warm spring day and we sat on some boulders in a front row seat for beauty. The tide was slowly creeping in and we sat watching it slither in. I found myself talking to it. Asking it how she could go away like that to return changed and more alive than ever. Asking her how she could go through something so traumatic to come back more beautiful and stronger than ever.

    She answered me with the crashing of the waves against the shore, each one vibrational and electrifying. The sound of the water hypnotizing the pain, easing it into submission and coaxing it for release. I never wanted to leave the beach, never wanted to be without her addicting voice. I started to hear the waves in my sleep, a soothing lullaby that allowed me to drift off into the blue light of night. The dreams came more frequently of him, more confusing yet comprehensible. I would hear his voice telling me to listen, I would wake to him calling my name. The dreams were not of what was him, but of what he was now. Forever the protector, forever the big brother.

    They made me think that maybe he was hurting too, and that he could not rest because I was not at peace. He came to me every night in my dreams, so vivid, so real. Sometimes not saying a word, just sitting with me until I woke. I often woke up to tears soaking my pillow. Trying desperately to go back to sleep to see him one more time, angry at the morning light of reality. An incredible cycle that repeated every day until I understood exactly what it was, I needed to do.

I needed to let the anger and rage go, but I was afraid. I was afraid to give up that control, afraid that if I let it go, then the world would see the pain it covered and the shame it masked. Afraid to allow anyone to see me exposed and bare. If I let go of anger and rage then I had nothing to shield the pain and anguish and I would be forced to deal with it. Forced to remove that too. The only way I felt that I could do this was to have help, but who? Who could possibly understand what it was I needed to do and have the resources to help me do it? A counselor, a stranger I didn't know. My husband, who could not even begin to imagine the pain I suffered, the trauma, the heartbreak?

'Take me to the beach', I would tell him, and he would with love and adoration. Never complaining how many times I asked, or how long we would stay. He would notice when I would walk away, and he would stay behind. I never questioned him on this, I suppose I knew the reason. I needed my alone time with the water. I needed the therapy she provided to me. I needed to lose myself in the rhythmic white noise of her waves against the shore. To hear her, to feel her power wash away the anger and rage so that I could sit with the pain, feel it, understand it, and learn how to let it all go.

3

Losing a loved one is never easy. Doesn't matter who it is. It places a vice around your heart and squeezes. Eventually we either learn to live it or we find a way to loosen its grip. The pain I felt when my brother died was none like I have ever felt before, compounded by the tumultuous life I lived and the stress I was under. The vice grip locked and rusted around my heart. One of the only people who could 'save me' from myself was gone. What could I do now but exist? I was doing that very thing extremely well. Going through the motions of every day. Slowly drowning. What better way to deal with it all than getting lost in water?

Memories flood your brain, like an invasion of ants, crawling over everything. Consuming anything in their path. No matter how much you try you just can't seem to separate them from anything else. Water seems to be the only thing that could disrupt their destructive invasion. Clearing them out so you can see what exactly it is that has a hold of their attention and rid of its contents. The problem is you can't just stick a garden hose up your nose and hope for the best no and I wouldn't recommend trying that approach either.

Getting lost in the tantalizing rhythm of waves is a better approach to flooding your nostrils with tap water. The pull of the moon to direct the flow, working in unison of the stages of the night to bring forth anything and everything that needs cleansing, including grief. For my 40th birthday I was supposed to take a cruise, but the pandemic saw to it that it was not in the cards to do so, so I settled for three nights on the beach. Just me, the cool crisp salty air and the water. My birthday falls in late September, so the air was not quite warm but not quite freezing either. I would say it was perfect.

By now I had survived 4 years without my brother and that is an understatement on just how well I had been doing up to this point. I was anything but ok, and the year I had spent in Maine so far was bringing it all to the surface. Not just his death, but everything. Every hurt, pain, traumatic experience everything! I noticed the effect dealing with myself had on me when I was able to host my mom for the summer prior to my birthday. The sheer fact she lasted a month with me is growth in and of itself. I had not yet forgiven her for what she had done, but I had taken responsibility for my part. I know people say that abuse and trauma is never the victim's fault, this is very true. But my reaction to it, my hatred, my anger, was just that, mine. I alone control nothing but myself. I can't control things that are done to me, but I can control how I respond to them. So, the growth I noticed in having her spend that month with me told me just how much time I wasted in my head.

So, for my 40th, I booked a hotel for three days about 200 feet from the shoreline. I opened the balcony doors and let the crashing of the waves sing their lullaby to me as I contemplated my next move. I knew I was hurting; I could feel it. I knew I had to stop because it was literally killing me. I just didn't know where to begin. Unaware that the work had already begun. There was an extra blanket in the closet of the hotel, so I took it with my beach blanket, and I headed down with my husband to the beach. The air was chilly but not overtly so. I picked a spot that sat in the setting sun and settled in to count my blessings that I made it another year.

As we watched the water, I started to feel the ache inside me come to the surface and struggle to get free. I didn't want to let it go. I wanted to hold onto it, wanted to shove it down into the abyss never to let it see the light of day. I was even more afraid than ever. Afraid that if I let it go, even just a little, I would indeed lose him completely as well. I was holding on to the notion that if I just stayed angry, stayed hurt, traumatized, that I could stay his sister. Not fully knowing that I would always be his sister and he my brother regardless if he were here in the flesh or not. I couldn't bear the thought of him fading into the abyss as well. Forgetting his face, his laughter, the sound of his voice.

The universe telling me it was ok was not good enough. I needed assurance, I needed tangible proof of that notion. I was not going to just accept it as true. My stubbornness and my incessant need for proof is a toxicity so fowl that the acceptance of that as well as the ownership of it, burned like pure grain alcohol on the back of my throat. Giving even the smallest inch could be fatal. At least that's what my survival brain told my heart. I have lived in complete and utter survival. Not living at all. Taking every hit to my heart, to my conscience, like a tank in battle. I had to, I had to be strong, I couldn't show weakness. I had people watching me, depending on me.

These thoughts ran rampant in my brain as the waves rolled in and out against the white capped shore. The sun setting and illuminating the sand and water in a purple hue, dancing on the water. My husband sat next to me and covered my shoulders with the extra blanket as the evening chilled the air even more. He never said a word to me. I loved that about him, He just lets me be and lets me talk when I am ready. Maybe he knew what was running through my mind, maybe he didn't. Either way he just sat with me and watched the water.

Each sway of the tide took me deeper into myself. I felt the claws of the hurt scraping my throat as tears swelled into my eyes. I just watched the water. I never took my eyes off of its glorious movement.

Against all fibers of my being, I let the tears burn my cheeks and kiss my lips. I whispered, *'You should be here.'* I closed my eyes to listen. I let the hypnotic roll of the waves flood my ears and carry me away. I let the flow take me to the hurt to the pain and I let the ebb take them away.

Healing from tragedy is rough, but healing from a lifetime of tragedy compounded with grief, is brutal and heinous. Hurting more to let it go, cauterizing the festered wounds, leaving beautifully placed scars. Never forgetting the pain, but no longer feeling it or living it. I have only just begun to heal, not quite to the scarred phase entirely. Not knowing which wound to tend to first, I decided to tend to the most recent and allow for that healing to take place.

I made, no I accepted, a decision to let go of anger and rage that September day on the beach. I decided to allow grief her proper place in the succession and accept her as priority. I did not realize until that night that I had not grieved. Truly grieved for my brother's passing. I had not even allowed the consideration. I spent years just angry, out of control, lost and sullen, that I did not grasp the gravity of the passing of my beloved brother. I was not honoring him. I was being selfish and ridiculous.

Forgiving others is easier than forgiving yourself. Acknowledging that you are in need of forgiveness from others is even easier than acknowledging it to yourself in the mirror. My brother would not have wanted me to carry on in the way I had been. He would say *'Rach, you of all people should not be doing this!'* Hell, he said it enough to me when he was alive, and well he would be right every single time. Never apologetic for calling anyone out on their shit, especially his sister.

The three days I spent on that beach, profoundly ground in just how heavy the ice brick was in my gut. Just how frostbitten I truly had become and how I was going to thaw from it all. I never truly accepted the fact that he was gone, I never truly accepted the trauma I experienced in my life so that notion makes sense that I would follow suit with the death of my brother. I was lost to my own device and the weight of it all was more than my armor could withstand.

Spending a year and a half in solitude, having the means to sit with myself as well as the courage, helped shed terrific light on everything that was dark in my life. The darkest being my brother's death. For the first time I started to breathe. I was still a stranger to one in the mirror, but I could breathe easier. I started to re-evaluate my life and my situations and began to make sense of it all. Tracing every wound, every scar, every hurt, with softer fingers. Really feeling each one gingerly with a new curiosity to really know them.

My whole world shattered under those blue lights that New Year's night, and every New Year's Eve when my husband and I celebrate another matrimonious year; I am constantly reminded that an amazing night ended with the tragedy of a new year. I could not celebrate the years with my wonderful husband, because I felt if I showed even an ounce of happiness, my brother would be forgotten. How selfish was I? How self-absorbed to think that my happiness could ever replace him?

Selfish to even consider anything above my own anger and pain. Letting go of all that, I was finally able to allow the tears to flow for my brother, for the life we had together, for the life he lived and for the mark he left on this world, on me. Living in Maine, as far away from anything that reminded me of him except myself. Trying to escape my own skin was futile, but damn it I tried. I tried to run as far and as fast as I could even though I was right on my own heels.

Grief settled in and she loosened the grip around my heart. She allowed the pain to well up in my eyes, get heavy and fall. She assured me that every time it would hurt, but when it was done there would be a masterpiece left where chaos resided. I was reminded that even though I was in control, I had to submit to her every time. The dreams kept coming, more of him just sitting with me in a room to ourselves. His million-dollar smile reflected in his eyes. Some, where he would talk to me, tell me that everything will be ok. Others he would show me glimpses of things I buried. My own personal guide to the blue light nights of my past.

JOURNAL ENTRY   28 JAN 2016
' had a rough morning driving to work. Songs making me think, cry. I hate crying. I heard his voice saying,' suck it up Barnes, we don't cry.' I turned on some heavy metal and rocked out. It has been getting easier, I think, maybe, hell I don't know. I've to stay busy, too busy it seems. Keep my thoughts random. My head is full of things to do next. I feel overwhelmed and anxious when I get still, even at bedtime it is hard to sleep. Mom makes it difficult to cope. With her meddling and incessant schemes. God, please help her. I want to believe her intentions are good, but when is enough, enough. I know what it is like to lose a child, the pain is unbearable, never goes away… Mike is and will always be a big part of me, there isn't a memory good or bad that he isn't in. I feel lost and disconnected. I hate how she can't see that. God, please help her.'

4

The very thought of not seeing my brother is still a hard pill to swallow to this day. I don't think there will ever be enough water to get it down without it stinging and scraping my throat and hitting my stomach like a ton of bricks. Every time my mother says his name, I still tighten my lips and tense up. I stopped talking to her, literally, for 6 months after my brother died. I was infuriated at her demeanor, her actions, her very essence, during that time. I was angry that I was completely blinded to her pain. I could have cared less. I was glad she was hurting, and I wanted her to suffer for it all.

I wanted her to feel every sting of it. I was satisfied when I didn't answer her calls or accept her pleas to other family members on her behalf. I wanted no part in it at all. I hoped that she was finally seeing the damage she caused and what it led to. I was amazed at the effort she put into trying to force her way back into my life. Overstepping boundaries. After 6 months I think I was just too numb to even care anymore, and I allowed her to come into my home only to have regretted that decision almost immediately. I was constantly shutting her down when she would talk about my brother, my dad, or anything I felt she didn't have a right to talk about. This led to her angrily leaving my house and another sporadic, even more volatile relationship with me. I didn't hate her, no, I was pissed at why she didn't try this damn hard from the beginning. I thought maybe, just maybe if she did, my brother would not be laying six feet deep in a cold, lonely grave.

Distance was not enough, she would always over do, over speak, over share anything going on with me. I felt violated and it just fueled my anger and rage even more. I blocked her completely from everything. Phone, social media, I stopped including her in my life, in my kids' life. Everything. The funny thing about that is, I didn't have to. She was never really a part of any of that, and my anger just sealed the deal even more so. I could not deal with the fact that she could not take responsibility for her part in it all. So consumed with that, I couldn't even take responsibility for my own shit.

Moving to Maine allowed, no, forced me to do that very thing. Forced me to recognize that anger and rage fueled hate and animosity and that gave birth to a vengeful appetite. An appetite so ravenous that it was never satisfied, and I consumed detrimentally. Slowly poisoning that which was me.

We all grieve in different ways, we all cope, deal, struggle, according to our own mind set. Some of us freak out, some withdrawal, some of us never deal at all. I think I am some of it all, that what I thought was healing and coping was really an illusion.

It wasn't until I sat across from her at my in-laws' table and I saw defeat on her face, that I knew the damage that had been done was done, and I was ashamed. I have never been an eye for an eye kind of person, or at least I fooled myself into believing that. And that was exactly what I had done to her. For all her faults, she did not deserve my wrath. If for the very least, the satisfaction of bringing me to her level. She deserved to grieve and heal and I was not the person to tell her she couldn't. In that epiphanic moment, I grew and healed a little more. The sting and taste of it is still fresh on my heart and tongue.

I have never not loved my mom or respected her, I was angry, hurt, and confused. I never could and still can't wrap my brain around why anyone would treat their children, their daughter the way I was. But it was not for me to understand, for I never could. It was for me to become better than that, to rise above it all and to make sure I broke the cycle. I did that by not raising my boys the same as I and I continue to do it by grieving the loss of childhood, my brother, and healing from it all.

The only thing I regret is the fact my brother had to die for me to see this. For me to actually deal with it all and heal. I noticed the fact that it took his death for my mom to realize whatever demon in herself to make changes, but I was too damn blinded by my own to do the same. It was almost like the glue started to peel in our family. My dad calls more, my other brother said, *'I love you Rach,'* more, and my own boys are closer. In a desperate attempt to hold what was left tightly together. So, what the hell was wrong with me? Me, always on the outside waiting to get in. So used to the cold, heat feels wrong.

    Being in Maine helped me to appreciate the cold. Not only literally with her brutal winters, but figuratively as well. When you are snowed in for days at a time you get creative, or you get cabin fever, and I did both. Creatively curing cabin fever was no easy feat, especially when left to your own devices and demons. I learned to accept what was and let go of what I could. Some things are forever embedded into you that letting go is not an option, so you get creative and adapt. We as humans are an incredible species and have perfected the ability to adapt to our ever-changing surroundings. I felt I was the one human who struggled with this. I thought I was the only one feeling this much pain, and that no one else could ever help, understand, much less possibly fathom what I went through and am going through. Adapting taught me I was wrong. It forced me to change how I spoke, how I reacted, how I grew and healed. I don't think I could have done this very thing had my actions not led me to a rural valley in Maine.

I remember the moment I let grief completely tear my soul apart and cleanse me of my hurt and pain for Michael. I was sitting once again in my car this time after work, and I was mesmerized by the full moon gallantly staring back at me. The most beautiful aspect of Maine to me is how close the sky is. Like I am on the top rung of the ladder to the heavens and all I have to do is stretch my arm out to touch it. This night the moon was so big, so bright that it lit the inside of my car and the surrounding area on the darkest street. I love all things moon related. I am truly in awe of his magnificent power. This night he was encased in clouds, but his magnitude towered over them.

I watched in pure astonishment, just transfixed on him and my eyes began to sting as I once again said, *"you should be here."* I thought I heard him say, *'I am'*, and a white-hot pain seared through my soul and erupted out of my body and flooded my cheeks. I did not try to stop it, I couldn't. I let grief take over and I let her tear it all down as I watched the moon through clouded eyes. I have no idea how long I sat in that car that night, but I didn't care. I needed the offensiveness of it. I have only ever learned the hard way, and grief knew that. She knew the only way to feel better is to cut it deeper. To go below the festered wounds and peel it away a layer at time. It is the only way to allow healing, to allow growth.

I look at the moon through different eyes now. My love for it runs deeper than ever before. I felt his collusion with grief that night so profoundly and understood their attack on my pain was strategic and well executed, pure and deserved. As much as I did not like it, it needed to happen. I was drowning in my own shit that was affecting my health, my home, my marriage. A cancer so out of control that it would take a miracle to cure, and I believe that night in my car with that massive full moon, I touched the very beginning of a miracle.

It only took one time to have me wanting that feeling of release. The electrifying sensation that coursed through my body, the feeling of being able to take a breath and not feel the pain so much, was more than enough to make me want to shed more, to heal more, to grow more. It was an epic realization of just how much pain I was in. I had let the cold settle and let it mask it all. I let it make me a zombie, a mindless, heartless, shell of a person. With that realization had to come acceptance and ownership. There wasn't any way around it.

I had to accept that he was gone, I had to own that I could not call him up just for shits and giggles. I had to accept that letting him go does not mean he is gone, it meant that I could go one without him and I would be ok. That everything he was to me, he still is. Everything he taught me I still knew and that everything from this point on, he has influenced. I was not honoring him; I was burying him. It was time to honor him and allow that hurt to heal so that I could start another cycle of grief, letting go, healing and growing. I had to own up to the hurt I caused in the wake of anger's destruction and make amends not only to those that I hurt, but more importantly to myself. My dad once told me, *'Baby girl, doing things for yourself is not selfish, it's self-care.'* I had to own that.

Healing is ugly, it is not rainbows and kittens, it is brimstone and fire. It is necessary in order to not fall into a bottomless pit and be suspended in nothingness. Healing from loss is even more so. The devastation I felt, I have no words to describe. I lost a child of my own and that did not strike me as hard as the loss of my brother. Maybe the combination of the two was just more than I could have imagined. Maybe it was because my baby was still born, where I had a lifetime with my brother. Whatever the reason, if there is one, left a wound so raw and exposed in my soul.

They say time heals all wounds; I say they are wrong. Time does not heal anything; it puts a band aid on it. It allows for the ability to shove it all down and keep moving forward, because that's what we do. I believe that 'in time' we either learn to deal with it or we learn to live with it, neither way heals. Healing needs to be grotesque and consistent. Like changing bandages every day from a bullet wound. Cleaning out the festering part, placing new bandages on it. Each time it heals more, each time it makes an atmosphere for a beautifully placed scar to form and one hell of a story to tell.

I know what stress and turmoil can do to a person, I never thought it would ever tear me down the way it did. I thought I could handle anything. I had survived some of the most vicious and unimaginable things and was even more sure I could handle the death of my brother. I was wrong in all the ways you can imagine. I mean, I handled his death in the same way I handled the trauma and other stress in my life. I sucked it all in, pulled my big girl panties up and I never let any of them see me cry. I never let anyone get too close afraid they would see the wounds, or worse smell the rot that had set in. Healing stepped in and said *hold my beer I bet I could shake some shit up.*

There is never a good time to heal, it is a necessity and will force its hand if need be. It is not something you prepare for. I have heard others tell me that *'when you're ready Rachael, you will.'* I was never ready. Pain is addictive. Healing means there won't be any more pain, right? Or that's what I thought. I found that healing doesn't take away the pain. The hurt I feel, I still feel to this day, it has been 7.5 years and there is still an ache in my heart. A memory of the ice brick that laid heavily in my gut. Healing allows me to write these words, although difficult, without pause or tear stained eyes. To talk about him with ease. To honor him as he should be honored and remembered. It has also allowed me to be more open about the other past traumas I endured in my lifetime.

I was not ready to allow anyone to see that side of me, not ready to see myself raw and exposed in the mirror. Some never heal, some fall victim to the addiction of the pain. I allowed my pain to be touched, to be comforted, to be bandaged and cleansed over and over again. It allowed me to feel more than the pain and the hurt. I gained a better respect for myself, for my brother, for all the blue light nights of my past and present. Tragedy happens, stress happens, I was not ready for a new way to handle those things when they do. Healing showed me a way.

My best friend sat in my car with me a few weeks ago, and just listened to my mouth ramble out what my brain wanted to say. I have always been the advice giver and never the taker. I have listened to those that have spewed their thoughts and opinions, rarely taking heed to what they had to say. Too damn stubborn to even consider it. That night, we sat in my car in her driveway and I, for the first time in the 24 years we have been friends, opened a door and let her see into that room of my psyche. She later told me that she was shocked and appreciative that I trusted her enough to tell her the things that I told her.

I never not trusted her. I didn't trust myself. I was comfortable telling her or anyone some of the things that I needed to say. Unsure as to why I was so afraid, I just was. I am still afraid, afraid that what I have to say will deter those I am opening up to, away from me. Afraid that my damaged and broken person will be too much for anyone to handle. I am learning this is a response to the trauma and not an actual occurrence. My dad tells me all the time,' *those that stay, stay, no matter what.'* I finally understood that that statement goes for me too.

    Healing did not and has not prepared me for any of it. I learn as I go. There are moments where I still need to be left alone. I prefer it, and that's ok. I get overstimulated and I need the time to regroup and refocus. The difference is, when I have had my moment, I can sit down with my husband, my friend, or even you the reader, and allow you all to see behind the door I needed time to open.

    The brother door was the hardest to open and even harder to close. I don't think I will ever completely close it, only time will. It still stings and burns a little where the frostbite took its toll. I respect the colder months more than I have ever before. It's amazing how certain events put a brand on your heart, how certain smells and sounds take you back. When Michael died, I stopped letting those things take me back. I stopped reveling in the nostalgia of it. I would scroll past pictures of him, turn off music that reminded me of him, stopped cooking things he liked to eat, stopped even mentioning his name.

    That was not healing or handling any damn thing, I was blinded by the ever-present survival of my life. I was numb to it all until that faith filled, full moon night when I was brought to my knees. Healing is brutal and rightfully so, and I think that is why we think we have to prepare for it. And why some of us never really heal from these things. Or at least that is my belief of the matter. I know I didn't and honestly, I can say that had I not succumbed to it, I probably would not be here writing this.

I have always wondered why I was even still here, wondered why there was not a second plot next to my brother's. I may never know the exact answer and it very well could be a rhetorical thought. I do know that looking back on everything it was my "I will show you,' attitude. My ridiculous obsession with proving people wrong. My outright stubbornness to be more than what everyone deemed me to be. I was super focused on making sure others knew I was just fine and doing everything they said I couldn't, that I failed to see the destruction I had created along the way. The song lyrics by Billie Joel, *'only the good die young,'* took on a whole new meaning when my brother died. He was 5 months shy of his 40th birthday. Although I am willing and ready to meet my maker when my time comes, I couldn't miss the subliminal message of those words.

I haven't been good, not by a longshot. Being a good person, always doing what is right, taking care of what needs to be taken care of, does not mean that I was 'good'. The anger, the hate, the pain, everything that is harsh to the tongue when spoken, I was wrapped up in. Slowly poisoning myself and everything in my path. Healing showed me the trail of casualties in my wake. A very hard image to see, an even harder reconciliation.

It showed me how I can go back and repair what I can and rebuild what I can't. It also showed me where I tried to repair and rebuild what I did not break and helped me to understand that I had to forgive myself for trying. The hardest of those was the death of my brother. That I had to let him go and let his maker do the repairs and rebuild, and that in his place I could do something, I could plant something new, something admirable and honorable to myself and to him. I read a quote by Audi Brown that says,`` *You are responsible for how long you let what hurt you, haunt you.*" I spent, no I wasted years not taking this responsibility. Not reconciling things that needed it and not putting others to bed that didn't.

JOURNAL ENTRY   30 JAN 2016
'...mind just wanders and I want to do is sleep, but at night I see him. God help to fade this from my sight. I know I can't erase it, but please can you help me to fade it enough so I can sleep'... 'I see myself getting angry quickly and not wanting to be around my boys or my husband. I feel consumed, claustrophobic, and restless'...

5

    I hate the phrase, *'oh you'll get over it!'* Like damn Karen, have a heart much. I remember after my brother's funeral, my dad attended the funeral of one of his family members and his sister, the mother of the cousin who was with my brother that night, saw my dad. He, being just as stubborn and it's where I get it from, kept his distance from her. Whether rightfully so or not, the death of my brother was still very raw at this time and my dad was very hurt and angry. She walks up to him and yells,*' he's dead, get over it!'* Now I was not there to witness this, however, several people heard her say this to my dad.

    I will never forget the look on his face as he was telling me this story. I have never, I mean never, seen this man cry much less break down in pure agony, at his own sister talking to him like that. I went back to my conversation with my brother where I told him I never wanted to see him again and I lost it. I had to leave my dad's place and I drove the hour and half back to my house in silence.

I told my husband about the conversation my dad had, and I remember saying to him,*' can you imagine saying something like that to your sister or brother?'* Big ass, spiked, pill I just swallowed right there.

These things you don't just reach into your head, fumble around in the dark until you find the switch and turn it off. Not how this works, believe me I tried. Never found that damn switch. What I did find was far more illuminating than any light could be, but that was after I sat in the cold dark. Looking back at all this, it was a wonder that I did not get lost in the thick of it. Perhaps I did for a time, pretending that I knew what I was doing and where I was going. Wandering around aimlessly in a poetic posture, giving the illusion I had my shit together. The fact being, I was only fooling myself. I was only putting on a show in my mind while the rest of the world saw a disastrous train wreck.

We can't take back words, but we can correct actions. I spent way too much time on the words I said to Michael just two months before his death, not wanting to accept the fact that his actions at my wedding corrected the actions of his sister. I was way too damn angry, I had to let that go before I realized that all was forgiven in that instance. I still have a hard time to this day. His birthday passed recently, and I felt off all day, but I did not cry nor was I angry. Just a little unsettled. That, my friend, is healing. Two years ago in Maine, I decided I wanted to do something for him and honor him on his 44th birthday. I bought 44 balloons and I had my husband drive me out to Marsh Point lighthouse in Maine. A beautiful lighthouse on a rocky shoreline of Maine. I had seen a picture of it and was drawn to its mysterious beauty and an electrifying feeling flooded my veins and I knew this was the place to let him go.

I took those 44 balloons and I walked alone down the long pier that ended at the lighthouse. I stood on the right of the door and looked out at the semi calm water. The wind was brisk that day causing small waves to lap over the rocks of the shore. A beautiful blue sky, fluffy clouds and a warming sun. I turned my tear-soaked face to the sun and closed my eyes. I whispered, *' you should be here, but I have to let you go. Until I see you again, I love you.'* The wind picked up and blew the balloons around my body. I smiled as I let them go. I stood there watching them float magnificently away. They lingered a moment almost as if he turned to wave at me and then soared towards the heavens. I felt this shift in my person and a shock wave roared through me, and I knew. I knew that I would never 'get over' his death, but that I could heal and have a life after his death.

I said earlier that time does not heal, time does allow for the space and opportunity to heal. I felt I was stuck in a time loop. Just repeating the day over and over again. The memories of that plagued my nights and infiltrated my days. I could not sleep and if I weren't occupied during the day, I climbed the walls. I had no clue this was not how grief works, all I knew was, if I'm busy I don't think and if I don't think I won't hurt and that's healing right? Apparently, my life up to this point says that is a lie. I couldn't just work it away. I couldn't stay occupied enough to even try. The sleepless nights were definitely taking its toll on me, and I was suffering more in the day from it. Something had to give and give it did.

   I said previously that healing was a bitch to be reckoned with and boy I thought I had her whipped. I couldn't have been more wrong. I am still transitioning, still healing and still hurting at the same time. It is a process, and it will take time, however, I no longer fight the lessons it is trying to teach me. I have a lot I need healing from, not just the death of my brother. I just prioritized the areas I needed to heal from starting with what I felt was the worst of them all.

   Michael David Barnes was born May 24, 1976, to a fifteen-year-old mother and an eighteen-year-old father. Babies themselves. His middle name is my dad's first name and if that isn't an indication, he was loved by them, I don't know what is. My mother was a very young and troubled mother and despite it all, I believe she tried as did my dad. Looking back at photographs of my brother as a baby he was a happy baby, or it seemed. I began to see his smile fade with each picture as his demons settled in. We will never know the pain his demons caused, but I felt it all, the day he died. I felt them scream in agony from my own lips. I felt them searching for their vessel that laid on the floor of that house. I heard their anguish as his maker took him home. I felt his pain leave his body and his soul rested.

The only comfort I took during that time was the fact that he was no longer feeling any more pain. That comfort has helped me get to where I am today. Almost a decade later, allowing you the reader a glimpse into my horrific healing from one of the most tragic blue light nights in my life. It is ironic that I lost my daughter in the middle of the night, my brother, and my grandfather. It was not until right now as I am typing this that I realized, damn what a way to go, in the presence of the ultimate light to guide them into their next life. The Moon.

He was charismatic, funny, and intelligent. He never backed down from anything; he always spoke his mind. He taught me to never be afraid of anything or anyone, including myself. He was a dedicated father and loved his wife and kids more than he loved himself. I hope they knew that, despite it all, I hope they do. He was my biggest fan and even harder critic. I always wanted his opinion and advice. I still seek it to this day. I still look to the heavens and ask him to hold my hand as I step off any cliff. He did not deserve any of this but I am sure glad he lived the life he did. I am so blessed to have known him in any context.

The circumstances of his death are suspicious at best. The coroner ruled that he died from an aortic aneurysm. Basically, the main vein of his heart exploded. He was dead before he even knew it. The 'overdose' theory was squashed with this revelation, however, the events of that night lead us all to believe that there is far more to this story. My relentless brain and my incessant need to know why has me to this day questioning everything. I am only saddened by the fact that he was treated poorly. He deserves to have justice. I know that his cause of death was basically 'natural causes,' but what about the manner? Where did the bruises come from the funeral director found or the suspicious behavior of my cousin? There are people that know the truth and that is all we as his family want.

No, we will never 'get over it.' Not with so many unanswered questions, but for me at least I now can process this in a better light, in a better mind frame. One free of the anger and the rage that consumed my life for so long. I can now sleep better at night. I now allow his name to be spoken by those I previously deemed unworthy to even think they could. I would not be able to do any of this had I not gone inside my head and pulled Rachael out. I am ok with letting my husband in to see the damage this has caused me and allow him to touch the most vulnerable places I had tucked away.

I didn't realize that I welcomed Michael's demons to take up residence with my own until I released them. That electric sensation I felt that May afternoon on that pier was grief opening their cages and letting them free. Am I still grieving?

Some. The tears on my computer as I write this are proof. Am I better than I was? No doubt. I will never forget when the moon and my grief colluded to attack my senses and beautifully forced me to let go. I have seen people hold on to such things and have seen the effects it has done to them, but I couldn't see mine. Not before that cold, full moon night in Maine.

The hardest thing a parent will ever do, but should never have to do, is bury a child. It is the most excruciating pain one can ever feel. The pain of losing my brother is tied with that. I am a rare breed and have the unfortunate reality of knowing what it feels like to lose both. I am getting better with every day. Time makes it easier, but not better. That is something I have to work at every single day. The sting of it lessens every day. I am now able to celebrate my anniversary with my amazing husband without anxiety, dread, or over sensitivity. I can now face each New Year's Day with honor and grace.

I no longer seek a New Year's resolution; no, I seek revolutions. I seek constitutional empowerment. I tackle a new pain every year. Yes, I said year. Each one needs its own time to grieve, time to heal and time to let go. Each year I get closer to a completely new Rachael. One that never forgets but lives and forgives. Forgives herself mainly and foremost. I cannot forgive others, if I cannot forgive myself for the damage I have allowed or caused. Forgiveness needs to be first inward before it can be outward. That too was difficult to swallow. The cold that set in 7 years ago, I can still feel, but it is felt only as a memory. One where I control the response or attention, I give it.

    Michael David Barnes died January 1, 2016, on a frigid Oklahoma night. He was with people he thought he trusted. His guard was down as he allowed his baby cousin to fill a syringe and slowly push the burn into his veins, excitedly waiting for the rush to set in so his pain would stop. He was unaware that she didn't do the same as I imagined she told him she would. The thoughts and details of that night still run rampant in my head, each scenario more sinister than the last. The hardest to accept, to heal from, is the unknown of it all. The uncertainty of what happened after he was shot up, after he decided to take a shower, after it all. That is the cold that set in and made itself a home in my soul and still lingers to this day. It has all but melted, aside from the portion reserved for the truth. That notion alone is a reason that I can't just 'get over it.'

    I do believe that she is responsible for his death. There is a difference between causing a death and being responsible. I do believe that there was a plan to maybe not mortally hurt my brother, but to hurt him, nonetheless. The drug world is a dangerous game to play, both for the user and the dealer and everyone else in between. I do not hate my cousin, I am angry, and I am hurt, and before I started to heal, I could have done her harm. She doesn't deserve that. I know that now. I know that will never bring him back and it would add more casualties to this senseless act. It took me a long time to get to this point.

   The police officers that night had her detained in the back of the cop car for her own protection that night. I was unaware of the threats being made to her that night. I was astonished at the implication that any harm would have been done to her, looking back now, it would have been me. When all of your sensibilities are gone, rationalization goes with it. It was me they were protecting her from. Me the hot-tempered baby sister who saw her as a murderer at that time. I never made any threats to her, I never said a word about it, but it would have been me.

   So, my New Years are a little different nowadays. A constant reminder of the cold that coursed through my veins, of the detrimental state I was in. I celebrate my anniversary and the complete revolution around the sun with a humbled spirit and clearer outlook. I spent an eternity in darkness, afraid of the light. What I have taken away from all this is that life needs to be lived now. Anger, rage, grief, they all have a time and a place, but need to be acknowledged, dealt with and then released. It is never a good thing to be stuck in any context, especially being stuck in the poisonous quicksand of emotion. These emotions I was feeling, am feeling, are all normal. What wasn't normal was my obsession and addiction to them. I let the cold infiltrate my veins and take control of my senses. I once again sought out anything to take the pain away instead of dealing with it head on.

I absolutely hate the phrase, *'that which does not kill, makes you stronger,'* No it doesn't. I was not strong; I was weak, and I was broken, and it almost killed me too. Trauma is not something to be glorified but recognized. It needs to be honored in a way of yes it happened, yes it broke me, and yes, I can rise above it all. I look around with my mind's eye at the ashes of it and I scoop it up in my hands and let it fall between my fingers like sand. I welcome it to come to the surface and flood my senses so that I can rid it from my body, cleanse my soul of the tar that bogs it down. I now honor that cold and respect its power, if I don't, I am useless against its pull. I accepted the death of my brother, and I am hopeful I will be successful in my pursuit of complete and utter healing. I love the moon more every time I see it. I like to imagine that when he causes me to look up at him and all his glory, my brother lounges on its edge, smiling that million dollar smile down at me.

My brother was laid to rest on January 8, 2016, surrounded by people who loved him, needed him, missed him. I did not attend his funeral, for reasons I will defend to this day, however, it was standing room only at the service and the gravesite was even more crowded. I can only hope to have such a following in my passing. My mom did a beautiful job picking out his casket and releasing balloons in his honor. The pictures that flooded my phone that day have me teary eyed to this day. It is still so hard when memories pop up on Facebook, or when I still see the pain run across my parents' faces. I now can look without turning away or quickly scrolling passed.

December of 2020, I read his obituary for the first time since he passed, while writing this. It hits a little differently now that his son is gone too. But there was something I noticed that I hadn't before. A link to plant a tree in his name. I thought, how odd to plant a tree, something that will die as well, but at the same time I thought how magnificent. It inspired me to do something for his daughter. I did not plant a tree. I planted a way for her to always have something to look up to. I had the moon and I wanted to give her the stars. I renamed a star her daddy's name and I sent it to her that Christmas. A gift her mother told me that made her cry happy/sad tears. Well, Caddiebug me too.

I hope that wherever he is, he is happy, he is free, he is living his best afterlife. I hope he knows that his baby sister will never forget him. She will never allow anyone to tarnish his name or his life. I hope he knows how much she loves him; how much she misses him every single day. I hope his son rests high with him and that he knows as well how much he is loved and missed. I hope his daughter never forgets the love he had for her. I hope she knows he would want her to live her best life however she wanted to live. I hope his ex-wife will always remember the good and not dwell on the bad and that she will always be family.

I hope my dad knows that he looked up to him, despite it all. I hope that Jeremy knows that he didn't come to see him locked up because he couldn't bear to see him that way and that he was Mike's hero in every story he ever told; and that my little brother knows that he was excited for him to be here. I hope my mom knows that without love there cannot be hate and that despite it all she was loved by him. I still carry a lot of his secrets and I will forever hold them close to me. I did not write this to hurt anyone, I wrote this for myself, for the love of my brother and for my own healing. I hope whoever reads these words doesn't feel my pain but honors it. I never want anyone to feel what I went through. The pain I felt was amplified by anger, rage, hate, everything dark is afraid of. I hope that having the courage to write this, to put it all on paper and to allow others a glimpse into my darkness, will help me to love the light a little more. To heal more, and if that helps anyone else, well then that is a perk in this process I suppose.

Six years, five months, and thirteen days, that is how long he has been gone so far, and I am so glad I got to spend his last night with him. I am so honored to have known him, to have loved him, to have been the one to send him home. I will always be Mike's sister. I grew up hating that nameless identity, I healed loving it. I still have my moments and days when I still feel the cold and tears stain my face. Those days when I miss him the most; the graduations of my boys, the wedding of my oldest, and all the other big events I still find myself reaching for the phone to call and tell him about. I still tell him, just not by phone. I walk outside on a clear night; I find my beloved moon and I tell him. I feel him the most on cloudy nights and the moon looks like it is resting on them. The nights where I am reminded of the pact my grief made with that celestial being that guards the night and forced me to my knees in surrender. The night I started to heal and rise above it all. The nights where the moonlight filters through the clouds, casting a blue haze on the night. Those nights I smile, close my eyes and turn my face to the moon and whisper, *'you should be here.'*

JOURNAL ENTRY   31 JAN 2016
...'I felt him today, his hand on my shoulder. It is comforting to know he is ok. He needs to know I will be ok as well and not to worry. I don't like letting other people know of these things. I try to fight them, but every once and awhile one will catch me off guard. I told him to go home, that he doesn't belong here anymore, and that he is free now'...

JOURNAL ENTRY   7 FEB 2016

"Today has been amazing so far. Haven't felt anxious or angry all day. Maybe I am just numb to it all, I don't know, but to not feel the way I have been, is a blessing that I will take in any context. I had a dream of him last night and saw him as if he were in the very room with me. I am still trying to make sense of it all... '

JOURNAL ENTRY   8 FEB 2016

'I don't like feeling antsy, can't sit still/ Always looking for something to do, never finding enough to do, or finding what would satisfy this emptiness. I am surrounded by people, but yet still so isolated. Isaiah caught me crying. I hate doing that in front of them, of anyone. It is a sign of weakness. When shouldn't I be, right? I know I need to let it all go, but when is it appropriate to do so?

JOURNAL ENTRY   11 FEB 2016

'How do I not have bad days? I try so hard not to, try to not let you being gone disrupt my life. You were my protector, my friend, my BROTHER. I counted on you . and you never let me down until now. TELL ME WHAT AM I SUPPOSED TO DO NOW? You taught me to be strong and independent, to face all my demons, but I failed to help you do the same. They are gone now and for that I am jealous of you.

Blue light night

Shadows in the night, darkness is too bright.
I want to see, but I am blinded by the powers that be.
Standing in a crowded room, noise fills the air.
All that surrounds me is silence, it's deafening,
and I am scared
I cry out to deaf ears.
I try to run, but I am stuck there.
I fall to my knees and there I stay.
It is there I begin to pray.
Grace is what I feel,
Remembering when I can no longer stand,
We are forced to kneel.
Seeking comfort in the light
From the horrors of that blue light night

The pain expressed in this piece, goes without saying. If this has hurt anyone, I am truly sorry. I needed this. I needed the healing it afforded me, the growth it gifted me and the closure. I hope that you all can take something away from this and I hope that those affected that January night, are healing. This piece was difficult beyond any words I can write or say. I am better now that I have written them. As private of a person as I am, I did something unimaginable in my life, and that has allowed others, you the reader, a perfect stranger, and those close to me, to see this side of me no one knew I had. The words in the journal entries are mine. It is the same journal I alluded to in these pages. It is not in its entirety as it is very private, but enough for you to see through the stained color glass I encased it in.

BLUE LIGHT NIGHT
By Rachael Hinkley

"There is no love like the love for a brother. There is no love like the love from a brother."
                -Astrid Alauda

Mike, your demons are gone now, may your light shine in death as your million-dollar smile did in life.
                Love Always, Rach

1

    Cold. Ever been so cold that it seeps into you like fire in your veins? It numbs you from the inside out, wrapping its icy fingers around your heart and throat, dumping a cube of ice in your gut to sit and wreak havoc on your insides. That is the kind of cold that only recently began to thaw in my soul. A cold darkness that settled in one January night and I doubt will ever completely leave.
New Years is supposed to be a time for renewal, resolutions, and revolutions. A time, we all deem the 'right time ' to change, the perfect time to start something new, but for me it was definitely a time to change. A change I was far from prepared to experience, a change that sent me on a roller coaster of starless nights. I hate roller coasters. Let me back up a bit and tell you about the events that led to one of the darkest and longest nights I have ever experienced, and I pray I never experience again. A month prior I received a phone call, one I had all too often received, late in the evening and I was annoyed at it. I had a long day at work and was not in the mood for whatever shenanigans this person

needed or wanted from me. Being the person I am, I answered. A scruffy voice asked me what I was doing, and I begrudgingly responded with,' *nothing, I just sat down from cleaning up after dinner, what's up?'*

"*Can you come pick me up?'* He asked. I let out a rough sigh and looked up at the clock on the wall. It was 9 pm and I really did not want to. I asked from where and he gave me directions. He then asked if he could stay at my house as he had nowhere else to go. I told him it was fine and that I would be there to get him shortly. I grumbled under my breath as I sat the phone down. My husband, who was my fiancé at the time, looked at me quizzically and I rolled my eyes and said, *"My Brother needs a ride, and wants to crash on our couch."*

We pulled into a parking lot of a laundromat and at first I did not see him and called him. The last time I saw him was a couple of months prior to this when I went to his house he was living at to retrieve some items I left. He was his usual crazy and chaotic self. I did not notice anything off or out of the ordinary, other than he was smoking synthetic weed. He asked me to take him to get more and I did. I always did. This night as I waited in my car on the phone to him, I saw a skeleton of a man stand up and walk towards my car. My jaw dropped as I hung up the phone with his.

"Oh my God!" I exclaimed. My fiancé asked what the matter was. I looked at him and pointed towards the man walking from the laundromat and towards my car. I watched him move in slow motion, methodically moving towards me. "Who is that?' My fiancé asked. "My brother." I sorrowfully answered. His dark set blue eyes were sunken in, he moved with pain but did not show it. His cheekbones were so prominent, they looked like they would cut through his skin and protrude out. His pants hung off of him, he kept pulling them up as he walked, despite wearing a belt. I took a deep breath in and let it out forcibly. "He's using again." I told my fiancé. "How do you know?' he asked. "Do you not see what I see?" I answered as my brother opened the back passenger door and slid into the seat behind my fiancé. I turned and looked at him. He smiled that million-dollar smile of his and immediately went into his, 'what's going on, Rach!' as he shut the door. I just looked at him and half assed smiled. I think he knew what I knew, and he said no more. I turned over the ignition and sat a moment looking out at the laundromat sign. I did not turn to him, I just looked out the windshield and spoke. "You will not bring that shit into my house and around my kids, do you hear me?' I demanded as I turned to look at him in his wide glassy eyes. He just looked at me and nodded his understanding.

We drove home to his incessant chatter of where he had been the last month. He told me of a drug-filled adventure and grand scheme to go to Arkansas and work with a buddy of his, and then decided to head to Nashville to try his hand at singing. He rambled on in an excited, manic, manner that made my already pounding head spin. I should have been used to this by now. He was always on a constant whirlwind between using and sobriety and sometimes they merged together. He was what we addicts call, a functioning addict. He would use it in order to work and work in order to use.

   They say marijuana is a gateway drug, but that isn't true. If we peel back the layers of an addict, we more times than not, find trauma. Drugs helped to escape the trauma and abuse I suffered as a child, and I cannot help but think that they did the same for my brother. I look back at old photographs and I used to focus on my own pain. You could clearly see running rampant across my face, and now when I see these old photos, I can see his. Pain he never spoke of trauma he never healed from. Just lost in the euphoria that burned through his veins, so he didn't have to speak or heal from. Sometimes, that is just easier.

   Growing up with him was an adventure in itself. He was forever the big brother, forever the protector and sometimes the antagonist. He was your typical big brother to a baby sister. Outwardly never wanting me to tag along, but inwardly glad I did. I found out later, through a slip up from him, he would make sure I was with him and my other brother, so I wouldn't be at the mercy of my abuser. Like I said, forever the protector. He never revealed too much to me, always stopping short of any explanation or details. As I got older, my own repressed memories filled in the blanks. He took a lot of my pain and all of his and held it in so tight that it consumed him in hate and grief. Always wondering why, I would ever help the one that hurt me. His only reprieve was the poison he pumped through his body, a notion I myself personally know.

   I have seen him sober, and I have seen him not, but what I saw that night I picked him up from that run down laundromat, I did not recognize. This was not brother; I have never seen him in such distress and disarray. I have seen and I have witnessed firsthand the devastation drugs can do to a person, to their body, to their demeanor and character. I watched my dad spiral as well as both my brothers, and I watched my own affair with hell slaughter the person I was meant to be.

   He spent a few days surfing my couch and when I say a few, I mean it. It only takes a few days for the pain to set in and the call of the craving screaming in your ears to make you move and seek out the relief it so desperately needs. He came to me one morning, sweating and eating everything in my house, a side effect of not eating or drinking for extended periods of time, wanting to borrow my car. I told him no, but that he could use my fiancé's truck. He swore it was to go do a plumbing job, and I believed him. Or maybe it was what I wanted to believe that is. Every fiber in my person screamed to not let him, tore at my conscience to not do the very thing I did, and gave him the keys to the truck.

The love for an addict is unbearable at most. It is difficult to maintain, it is heartbreaking and detrimental to the whole of things. The love I had, no have, for my brother runs deeper than any other I have encountered. I hold his secrets in my person, forever under lock and key. It was his love for me that overpowered the common sense to show him tough love and say no. I was so blinded by that, that I went against my own sobriety sometimes and caved under the pressure. Afraid that I would lose the very person who fought and saved me so many times, it was only fair that I do the same, right?

Unknowingly so, or perhaps turning a blind eye, not wanting to see the forest for the trees, I once again gave in. The promises he made fell on semi-deaf ears. With addicts the promises become thrown around like glitter, cluttering everything and serving no purpose. We hold onto them thinking maybe this time they mean it. Goes back to love tainting our visions and clouding our judgment. But when is it enough? When do we lift the veil and take off the blinders? When do we take our own lives back and realize this type of love is toxic to you both?

Three days later is when I did. When I got a phone call from a police officer wanting to know if I knew the person who was driving my fiancé's truck. He didn't have a driver's license and he was high. They were going to have to impound the truck and wanted to know if I could come get him. I think I said several hundred explicit words and told the officer he could call someone else because I was not coming to get him, and I hung up the phone. Two days after that, my car dealership called, pissed they had to go get our truck. Two days after that my brother called, I couldn't tell you what he wanted, I didn't care. I had had enough. I was infuriated and I told him so. I told him I never wanted to see him again, to not call me anymore, that I was done with his shit, and I hung up the phone. I blocked him on everything. Yes, I was that mad.

Yes, I caught hell for it too. I did not care, I was done. It had been me to answer the calls, me to go get him all hours of the night, me to write to him and accept phone calls when he was in prison, me to keep his secrets from his wife when he would call me to 'hook him up,' because I knew people. It had been ME and I was done. He would try to reach me any way he could. Hurt, no doubt, that his baby sister shunned him. I stuck to my guns, and I did not talk to him, I did not see him, I did not entertain any aspect of the liking. I did not see I would regret that decision to this day.

It hurt me to tell him these things, it tore at my heart something fierce. But I could not do it anymore, I could not watch him spiral into nothingness, I just could not do it. It was not for lack of love for him, or the want to help him, it was a lack of love for the choices he made in his life that led him to this destruction. I saw him start to decline six months prior and I ignored it, I shouldn't have. I justified it, I rationalized it, I said well 'it's just weed', then it went to,' it's just synthetic weed, it's legal you can get it anywhere.' These are not the justifications or validations that solved anything. I kick myself as I remember a moment standing in his den with him, his son and girlfriend. I was shaking my head at the fact that he was smoking with his 16-year-old son at the time when his son turned blue and was gasping for air. He slapped him on his back, and I rushed over and laid him down. Having to revive my own nephew as his father stood idly by too fucked up to even comprehend what was happening makes my stomach turn this very day. You would think at the moment he realized what the hell just happened that that would prompt him to stop.

I had no idea the 'it's just weed,' was far more than I anticipated. I never thought he would fall back into the harder shit. He vowed to not do anything heavier than weed when his son was born, and for the most part he held onto that partial sobriety. I am not trying to drag my brother and his illness through the mud, I am only offering some context, some sort of understanding into this tale that is anything but that. If not for my own understanding into the why of it. I cannot speak on what transpired in his life the years I was not there, dealing with my own hell, but I am not here to speak on that. I am here to talk about a sister's love for her addict brother, and the moment the cold took over my soul.

A month after the truck incident, I was preparing the final touches on the most wonderful day of my life so far. A day second to the birth of my boys. My wedding day. Even though I had been married previously, this one I wanted. This one I will keep forever. A day and night forever ingrained into my psyche fighting over where to file it under, joy or sorrow. Turns out, it would be both. I was busy with RSVP's and making sure every detail was perfect. I learned my brother was staying with my dad and I called my stepmom to confirm they would be ok to drive as my dad had trouble riding long distances in the car. I heard my brother's voice and asked my stepmom if he was there. Ever the hot-headed stubborn ass I am, she asked me if I wanted to talk to him, and I said no but asked her if she would ask him if he were going to attend the wedding. Yes, I know not very Jesus of me to stoop to high school level bullshit, no excuse, I did, I was petty, angrily so. He confirmed he wouldn't miss it and I left it at that. I continued with my wedding festivities and focused on the task at hand.

December 31, 2015, nationally marked for the end of an era and the precursor to a new, a day of chaos, joy, mishaps and laughs. A day I will forever cherish, not just for the pure excitement of finally being with a man who loved me in all the right places, or the fact that two families joined together made up of blood and oil, but also for the images I chose to hold onto of my brother. I spent the better part of the day running on coffee and adrenaline with my cousin and soon to be bonus daughter doing what I suspect most brides to be do before they take that walk down the aisle, hair, nails, and of course waxing eyebrows and mustaches. I had a private session later for my hair and makeup, but my cousin and bonus daughter needed to shine as well. My cousin was one of my matrons of honor, I had two, and my bonus daughter was just going to look beautiful regardless of the fact she had no role in this shindig. I was nervously excited, and anxiously, worried. Yes worried, I mean what could possibly go wrong right?

   Everything thus far was on schedule and according to plan. I had a few kinks to work out, but I was not worried about it. It would get handled or it wouldn't, I was more concerned with getting to the venue and putting myself together for this event of events. The greatest day of my life was about to commence, and I was as ecstatic as I was nervous. I could not shake the heaviness I felt in my stomach, the foreboding naw at my neck. I chalked it up to wedding day jitters and looking back…well hindsight is always 20/20. I sat surrounded by friends and family in a conference room of the venue. Clothes, shoes, hair care products, and make-up strung everywhere. Lighter exploding as everyone talked and carried on, excited to be here with me and sharing this day with me. I have never in my life had so many people turn up for anything I have ever done. Not a graduation, not a baby shower, nothing and I was amazed at the fact that everyone I invited came and then some. The room I was in was packed and I would soon find out so was the rest of the place.

My mom came strutting in as she always had to be the center of attention and the look on her face told me she knew she was not and I should have known then what shit she would cause, but this is not a Debra show tale. Not entirely though. I asked her one thing and that was whether or not my brother was there. You see I have three brothers, two older and one younger. Now I love my younger brother, he is more of a son to me than a brother as he is only two years older than my oldest son, but my older two, they hold a place in my heart I have yet to find a match to. My middle brother was not able to attend my wedding. A fate he himself sealed and was serving the time needed to rectify that mistake, so despite my anger towards my oldest brother, I wanted, no I needed him there. I could not shake for the life of me why the need to see him was so great. I mean what he did, and the anger I felt, why would I care if he showed up to this thing, right?

But something tugged at me something fierce, and it did not subside until I saw his face. I walked down the aisle and scanned it looking for him, I saw pictures later of me looking distraught as I walked hand in hand with my dad to meet the man who would take me from him, and I did not realize the weight was showing as I looked desperately for my brother in the sea of eyes that were on me. The feeling subsided a little as I watched the man of my dreams catch my eye and held me there as I walked up the steps and into his hands. I held his stare as everyone settled into their seats and all my focus was on him and the words of the chaplain. My whole body was shaking and as I repeated the words the Chaplin said to me, tears flowed heavily down my cheeks and smeared the horrendous makeup job, making it almost bearable. That is a story in itself, another time though. I closed my eyes and kissed the man before me as everyone clapped and stood and cheered a new couple into existence. As we walked back down the aisle as man and wife, I once again scanned the crowd for those deep-set blue eyes and that million-dollar smile. I did not voice my concern to anyone, I simply began to let the disappointment of him not showing up to set in. The photographer gathered everyone around and began to take his preplanned photos of the families and friends. He stood me up with my youngest brother at the altar, and as he posed us, I looked up and down the aisle came my disheveled, wide eyed, tucking his shirt into his pants that he probably threw on while in the car, brother. He saw me and flashed that million-dollar smile and practically ran the rest of the way to me. He was lit and it showed in his glassy eyes, but he was there, and that is all that mattered at the time. I wanted to recreate a photo we did at his wedding and so I posed him and my younger brother on either side of me and had the photographer take the picture. One I will covet and not ever give up to anyone.

Sitting at the wedding party table after the first dances and the food was served, he walked over to me and sat down beside me. I looked at him, still angry but glad he finally showed up. No words were exchanged, he just scooted the chair closer to me, smiled at me and rubbed my back the way someone does for comfort. I smiled back and leaned into his sideways hug, and just like that all was forgiven. Call it divine intervention, call it fate, call it whatever you want, I called it rectified. No one knew the events that would transpire after, no one could have predicted it, but looking at it now, I think I did. I think the nagging, insufferable feeling I had was more than wedding day jitters. I think the excitement of the day tangled in the premonition and clouded its clarity and I simply did not see.

I recall asking my husband 'Why didn't I tell him to come home with me?' and 'Why did I let him leave?' Answers to which he had none. Looking back, I am not convinced it would have made a bit of good if he had come home with me that night, not convinced that I would have been able to change his fate. I believe in predestination, and I believe we all have an hourglass of life and when it has run out of sand, we can't just flip it over. No matter how much we may want to, we can't interpret, disrupt, or change anyone else's life, path or journey, we are only in control of our own, and honestly, not even then.

We were set to take a cruise for our honeymoon. An adventure neither of us had ever partook, we were both excited to leave and we were due to set sail in three days. New Year's Eve was quiet in our home, we chose not to attend the after-party festivities of ringing in the new year with our friends and family and decided to just rest at home with our kiddos. We left the clean-up of the establishment to some of the patrons, and we took our leave as husband and wife back to our home. It was already an eventful day and night and others saw to it to make sure we ended with the unveiling of wedding gifts. I half expected my brother to show up with the rest of them at my house, but I was told he was taking my nephew home. He had accompanied his dad to my wedding, and I was happy to have him there with his girlfriend, missing his sister and mom. My brother was divorced from their mom, but she was still family nonetheless, and she continues to be to this day. I was not upset that he did not, I was relieved actually as I already had a houseful and did not want any more than that. After the gifts and the crowd left, the house was quiet. I remember it being eerily quiet. The exhaustion from the day did not allow me to ponder on the fact of a strangely quiet house and I went to bed next to my new amazing husband.

I was plagued with dreams, and I tossed and turned all night. Unable to make sense of the dream, I have tried so many times to do so, but it was gibberish at best. Fluttering images of my childhood mixed with events of my life, and images of my brothers in places I did not recognize. I woke earlier than normal and grudgingly got up to a sickening feeling in the pit of my stomach. Again, unsure as to what it was, I simply tried to shrug it off and I went about my day with preparing for our cruise. My husband had to work that night, and as I spent the day doing housework, I was folding laundry on the couch with my middle son watching T.V, mainly for background noise. The phone rang.

My mom came on the line and asked me if I had heard from my brother that day. I told her not since the night before at the wedding. She asked if I would call him as he was not answering her calls. Little side note, he rarely answered her calls if ever. She expressed to me that there was a rumor going around that he was injured, and I remember telling her,' *Mom, do you hear yourself, a rumor? Come on now, he is probably high somewhere, but I'll call.*' So, I did and did not get any answer as well, I left a voicemail, and I sent a text. I called my mom back and let her know that I did not get an answer either but that I left a voicemail and text and would let her know if he responds. She replied with,' *well your aunt called and told me he was dead. Can you call your cop friend and ask if he would run his name?*'

Annoyed, I said I would, and I called him to ask if he would run his name, he said he would and would call me back. I no sooner hung up with him when

my mom called again telling me that I needed to go to this address and tell the paramedics he was my brother. Confused as to what she was telling me, I asked several times *'what do you mean?'*
I will never forget these next words, ever. She answered,*' I don't know what happened, all I know is Summer called her mom to ask her what she should do, and she told her to call 911. They have been working on your brother for 30 mins now and need someone to go identify him.'*

    The guttural scream that escaped my body woke the dead. My son who was sitting next me jumped up as I threw my phone and went tail spinning into the kitchen, and he caught me as I went down and carefully placed me on the floor. Everything after that went black and I became robotic, unbelieving of what I just heard. My son took the address down that my mom tried to give, and he walked over to where I was still sitting on the floor and yelled at me to get up and go. I remember looking up at him and taking the paper and my phone from him. My mom was still on the line, I did not speak to her again. I hung it up and began calling my husband at work, as he had the only vehicle we had at the time. It was already dark, about 8 or 9 I cannot tell you which. The concept of time simply vanished from my mind. Still trying to call my husband I rushed over to the neighbors and asked them if they would take me to get the truck from him. I gave them a brief rundown of the situation and they quickly rushed me over to his work. At his work I angrily yelled for him to give me the keys as my mom called his phone to tell him to not let me drive. Yea that didn't work, nice try though. I took his keys as my aunt called telling me not to come that she was already headed that way. For the first time ever, I cussed at her. I told her. *'Fucked that, he is MY brother, I am on my way."*

That drive was the longest drive I have ever taken, no traffic, late at night, and speeding, still felt like an eternity to drive 15 miles. The whole way there I just kept repeating over and over again, *not my brother, not my brother, please God not my brother.* Not even paying attention to the road, oblivious to any cars on the road. It is a wonder I did not wreck; it is a miracle I did not get stopped for going 90 miles an hour. I later found out that my amazing cop friend cleared a path for me, told me he radioed my truck in and the situation. He even assigned himself to work the scene even though it was not his area to patrol.

I caressed a curve and slid to a halt behind three cop cars, blue lights lit the desolate area, illuminating the street in flickering chaos. I jumped out of the truck, I did not even shut the door, I don't even know how it got shut or who did it. I started running the minute my feet hit the pavement. My aunt and uncle, already there, as well as my cop friend. I ran, I managed to dodge my aunt and uncle as they tried to stop me. Only to be almost clothes lined by my cop friend and one other policeman standing there with him. I crashed into them; my friend held me there a minute as I fought against his hold. My aunt came up to us and he sort of shoved me into her. She held on to me as she told me," Rachael, *it's him, he's gone."* And I went down screaming, she held on to me as we both went down. My uncle hoovered over both of us.

  I started screaming at my friend to let me see him, he tried so gingerly to calm me down, but I wasn't having it. I screamed at him that I needed to see for myself it was him. He took a deep breath and yelled,*' I AM NOT LETTING YOU DO ANY DAMN THING UNTIL YOU CALM THE HELL DOWN!'* I went silent, he asked me once more if I was going to stay calm and I nodded as he helped me up and walked to the door of the house where my brother laid dead. He stood in the doorway and told me that I could not go any further than that. He had to get permission for me to even go that far.

  He held out his hand and told me it would be alright and led me into the house. The first thing I saw was a small TV leaning against the wall that faced the door and the smell of asphalt hit my nose. Drug houses have a distinct smell to them. The stench seeps into the floors and the walls and no amount of cleaning will ever get the smell out. But this house had the familiar smell of melted asphalt and pennies. I did not want to look away from the TV or the wall, I remember thinking how odd it was for a TV to be plugged in and leaning against the wall facing the door. It was just a weird scene. He assured again that it would be ok and held out his hand and placed it on my shoulder in an awkward show of comfort. He said, *'look Rachael, is that your brother?'* There lying prone in the middle of the floor, a bulb bag tube sticking out of his mouth, naked aside from a small cloth covering his groin, laid my brother. I told my friend that it was indeed my brother and as if he knew what I was about to ask, he said, *'No Rachael you can't go over there."* He led me out of the house, back into the blue lights of the night. My aunt was standing in the same spot I left her in, she watched me with tear-soaked eyes as I came solemnly down the stairs and stood in front of her. No words were needed, for she saw what I saw, and she was feeling what I was feeling. She just hugged me, held me there for a moment and then asked if I wanted to sit in her car to warm up.

 My aunt and I have a bond like no other, one forged from trauma and sealed in love and that January night, it became forged in an unforgettable, infallible, fire. One that has strengthened what we already had, one that we share separately but hold equally. One where, when I look at her, I no longer see my aunt, no, I see myself standing in the cold of a blue light night.

 I cannot tell when my parents showed up, all I can tell you is my mom was there before my dad. We all stood outside that house waiting for the medical examiner to come and get my brother. My friend would not let anyone in the house as it was an active crime scene. He did tell me however some of the events that went down that tragic night. My baby cousin was the one to call 911, but that I feel is the only good thing she did this night. According to police recollections, I say recollections, because the police report told a completely different story; My cousin and her boyfriend for lack of a better term, were in the house with other drug users, who I cannot say. They scattered like roaches in the light when the cops showed up. According to my cousin, she said she shot my brother up, but did not use any of what she gave my brother herself, even though she had been before this incident. She said that afterwards my brother complained of indigestion and was going to go take a shower and lay down. She said he went to the bathroom, heard him turn on the shower and then heard him yell out. She went to check on him and found him on the floor of the bathroom. She said she panicked and called her mom, who instructed her to call 911. In which she did. The amount of time she talked to her mom, I cannot tell you, there are conflicting stories, but I do know her mom kept telling her to get off the phone with her and call 911.

According to the police, when they showed up my cousin was cleaning up the house frantically and they found my brother on the floor of the living room. The fact that she was cleaning and did not run with the others in the house threw everyone for a loop, so much so that the cops detained her, put her in handcuffs and placed her in the back of a squad car. I was told that they were looking for anything to arrest her as her story kept changing as the events of the night. The true, true story lies with my cousin and my brother and well two can keep a secret if one of them is dead. There is room to believe she gave him a hotshot, but again only she can say what actually happened that night.

   Confused by this, I could not bring myself to walk over to the cop car and talk to her through the partially rolled down window. My family members tried but she just kept saying she didn't know what happened. When the medical examiner finally showed up the cold had set up residence in my soul and I am still unsure if I were numb from the below freezing temperatures, the pain, or both. I learned that they could not move my brother's body until the medical examiner got there as she is the authority in these situations. She is the one to say the manner of death and whether or not foul play may or may not have occurred.

   My mother had already arranged for the funeral home to come get my brother, but she did not have the authority nor the right to do so. She was quickly told that even the funeral home has to wait on the M.E. My mother would put on an extravagant show of bullshit from this point on. The police secured the house and closed the door once the medical examiner was on the scene. They had already been keeping people out of the house, but the door had been opened partially up to this point. I stood in the middle of the yard watching the house, unaware of the cold, of the people around me. My mom had offered me a blanket and I declined it. I did not want to be touched, bothered, nothing. This notion offended her, and she threw the blanket in my face, prompting my Granny to scold her daughter.

I heard a commotion behind me, and I turned to see what was going on, and I saw my dad walking up the road and I bolted, nearly knocking him down as I slammed into him sobbing, *'he's dead daddy, he's dead!"* He held onto me as we both walked back to the yard, my mom started screaming at him, unsure as to why. Her oldest sister and nephew grabbed her and held onto her as she hysterically sobbed. I have no doubt she was in pain, none. Losing a child is one of the hardest things a mother can go through, I myself have buried one, however, you will soon realize my angst. My dad let go of me and went to my mom, my brother after all was their oldest. She let him console her for a hot second before my stepmom came over and she literally pushed my dad backwards with enough force he stumbled.

I went over to where my cop friend was standing and I asked him if he could make sure that my parents did not see my brother that way, to ask if the M.E would cover him. He did that very thing, and they wheeled my brother out in a black body bag that was lit up with the blue lights of the night. My mom asked the M.E if she could see him and she promptly told her NO. This infuriated my mom and she yelled, 'BUT I"M HIS MOTHER!' This did not sway the M.E or her techs as they put my brother in the back of her van. My mom tried to get some information out of the M.E as she closed the back door of the van and maneuvered around the crowd of people surrounding it. My mom told her that the funeral home was in transit and was quickly told that they can turn around until after the autopsy. The M.E had enough suspicion and evidence that this was more than an accidental overdose.

   Here is where I will say this, the events of that night are scattered as there were multiple people there and each of them have their version of that frigid night, and this is mine. I do not care who it upsets, I do not care who this offends, I do care that my brother died in vain, he suffered in life. Plagued with demons of his own making and ones he tried to conquer. He took every hurt, every pain, every triumph, every burn in his veins, everything he tried to keep me safe from, to his grave. The events of that night were nothing but suspect and deemed a further investigation and when it was all said and done, he was just another junkie.

   When the M.E took my brother away we were able to go into the house and only retrieve belongings of my brother's that were in plain sight. If we could not see it, we could not take it. My mom and I were allowed to go with the accompaniment of my dear friend. The first thing I noticed when I re-entered that dreadful home was a blood stain where my brother was laying. Not where you might expect a bloodstain to be. It was in the place where his back was, high up by his shoulder blades. The image of my brother lying there will haunt me for all my days, so the bloodstain was not where it should be. If he had a heart attack, like they thought he had, why was blood there in that particular spot. I moved from the living room down a hallway looking at the floor. The floor was dry, free from any evidence of moving a wet, apparently bloodied body from the bathroom to the living room, and why was he in the living room if he fell in the bathroom? The hallway was wide enough for paramedics.

In a back bedroom I found my brother's clothes strewn around on a bed, his wallet laid on the floor next to his phone. My brother would not have walked butt naked from bedroom to the bathroom, he was notorious for leaving his wallet in his pants along with his phone. Wallet empty aside from his driver's license. We gathered his things there in that room. A small milk crate held his work boots and some tools, my mom tried to go through drawers but was quickly told she could on get what she could see. We both walked out of the room and into the bathroom. Into a pristine bathroom, free of any water, debris or splatter. The shower looked as if no water had ever graced its tub or curtain, no water on the floor, no wet towels, nothing. I have never seen a cleaner bathroom, especially in a known drug house.

That is when I remembered my cousin was cleaning the house when the paramedics showed up and I told my mom that very thing when she commented on the bone-dry bathtub, a detail she did not know up to that point. As we walked back out of the house, my mom was on a mission to have the head of her formal baby niece. My cousin was the daughter of my dad's baby sister. My mom wanted her to be charged and was infuriated at the fact that she was not being charged. She went on to yell obscenities and say things like, *'she had a hit out on him.'* Now I do not know if this statement is 100% accurate. All I have to go on is the story my brother told of an incident where he was attacked by a guy, we all thought was his friend. He rambled on about it being a set up, and well no one has ever confirmed or denied this accusation. Is it possible, sure, anything is possible? Now I know I just painted a very gruesome picture and well it was quite raw in nature and that is just how I tell a story, honest, raw, somewhat offensive, but I always come back around with something good.

    My brother was more than his addiction. He was an amazing big brother growing up. Almost like a father figure. He did not allow anyone to mistreat, disrespect, hurt or harm me or my middle brother. Sure, there were fights all siblings fight and argue, but we three were and still are very close despite the turbulent childhood we had. My brothers were star athletes. I loved to watch them both play football and have attended every single game they ever played. Michael, I know I have not mentioned his name before it is hard to even say it, was phenomenal, a football prodigy, I had no doubt he would have gone pro had the devil not got a hold of him.

He was charismatic and could charm the pants off anyone. He had a million-dollar smile that got him into just as much trouble as it did out of trouble. Intelligent beyond means, he was once suspended from school for fighting for a month, came back and aced a Trigonometry test without even being prepared for it. He was funny and loved to laugh but had a fire in him you didn't ever want to see. He did not want kids, true story, he was afraid he would treat them how we were treated growing up and he couldn't see doing that to anyone else. However, he was an amazing father, despite being smoking buddies with his teenage son. He adored that boy and even more so his daughter. He often would say he saw his sister in his daughter when she would pick on her older brother. This always got a laugh out of me and a "that's my girl!' My boys were adored by him as well, he would light up every time they were in his presence and they returned the adoration.

Addiction just does not destroy the body, but it infects and infests everything in its wake. It destroys all that was once an amazing person and turns it all black and leaves it to rot. The loved ones hold on to the person that is underneath it all. Hoping and praying that one day they will make it to the other side of it all and have one hell of a story to tell. The unfortunate truth of it all, the ones that do are a rare breed. I am only typing this as a reminder that I was one that made it out alive. What I have left of my brother are the memories and every now and again I see him in my now oldest brother, my boys, and myself when the light hits me just right in the mirror.

    The night of his death, it shook me so violently that I spun out of control and six months would go by before I even started to recover from it. When everyone left the scene, I was the last to go. Gently being coaxed by my cop friend to leave. I sat on the porch of that death house, and I was lost in the blue lights dancing against the early morning night. I was numb from inside out, just lost in the whole world. I do not remember being walked to my car or getting in or driving home. The house was eerily quiet when I returned, every soul asleep or at least in their rooms, I could not tell you if they were asleep or not, my guess is, no. My husband laid awake in the bed and did not say a word to me as I laid down next to him. He covered me up and held me gently. I did not realize that I was almost hypothermic being in the cold unprotected. I left the house the night before in flip flops, a sweatshirt and leggings in the brittle Oklahoma January cold. I was oblivious to it, my mind shut down every receptor to any physicality of my being. I could not discern cold from numb or numb from heartbreak.

    It was not until I started to shiver under the warmth of the blankets that I realized my core was frozen, my husband, being the ever-ready soldier, stripped his clothes off and mine and laid skin to skin with me until the shivering stopped. He never said a word, just held me close and rocked me gently. I must have fallen asleep out of sheer exhaustion because a vivid dream woke me two days later. I still remember it to this day six years later. *I am on a road trip, destination unknown, in a car with my middle brother and we come to this drawbridge. It was down and we began to cross as the waters rose quickly around us. The bridge started to rise and so did the water. It surrounded our car, and we began to shift against the raging current. Jeremy, my middle brother, jumps out of the car and onto the hood of it. He holds out his hands and yells, 'Stop and be still!' The water stops and plummets back into the ocean and recedes back to a calm flow of waves against the shore as we start to move across the bridge. Jeremy crawls back into the car and tells me, "It will be ok sis, I got you!"*

    It was so vivid and clear, it jolted me awake. I woke to a bright sun beaming through the window and on my face. I remember blinking against it as the light engulfed me, I laid there replaying the night before in my head. I later learned I had slept for two days straight. Every chance to rouse me was futile. I did not eat, but there were cups on the bedside table so I suppose I did drink, though I cannot recall. There isn't much I recall in those six months I was lost wandering into the abyss, except darkness and confusion. The cold still sitting heavy in my gut, the blue light night stuck on repeat running savagely through my brain. I remember the look everyone gave me as I emerged from my hole, the look of surprise and pity but mainly of loss. Loss of words to say or of any comfort they may try to offer. They walked on eggshells around me, unsure as to what to do or say.

My oldest asked if I were O.K and I simply nodded and walked over to the fridge. I remember standing in front of it holding the door open and being swallowed by the yellow light that glowed from it. Looking for something and nothing at the same time. Everyone still watching me as I closed the fridge and went back to bed. My husband walked into the room and stood there watching me. He asked if I was hungry, I said no. He stood there awhile; I could feel his stare on me as I watched the ceiling. I rolled over and went back to sleep. Images of my brother fluttered behind my eyelids, I would continue to have dreams of him talking to me, visiting me. Dreams not of the past, but as if he were still here. Dreams I came to cherish and would mourn when the morning came.

I did not attend his funeral; I was outright furious at the spectacle my mom made of my brother. She did deplorable things that I have only just begun to forgive her for. The decision I made to not attend his funeral I would be lying if I said it was a bad one, but it was not. It was a decision I made to honor the brother I knew, not the one that was being paraded around to suit the needs of an incredulous person. I do not hate my mother, no, I feel sorry for her. I was stricken with grief and anger, and it fueled animosity and the outrageous charade she put on during this time of horrendous anguish, I have deemed grievous at best. I have no doubt she was hurting, but I also know the performances she puts on to have the attention focused on her. This is not a tale to bash my mom, no, it is simply a sad truth in the thick of it.

The death of my brother affected us all tremendously and I personally know what it is like to bury a child, so looking back at my anger at the situation, I find myself ashamed. Ashamed of how my grief treated people. Ashamed of how I cursed everyone around me when all I wanted was understanding and comfort. Ashamed at the words I spoke to undeserving people, ashamed that I lost one of the only people who loved me unconditionally, and I pushed him away like garbage. I was angrier with myself than I was with anyone or anything else. I came to believe that the last night I saw him, the universe knew it would be my last. I think I kind of knew it too. The churning in my gut, the anxious wait for him to show up, I have never cared whether he showed or not, but that night I did.

I tried to go back to some form of normality. Some form of busy and preoccupation so I did not have to deal with the emotions that were wreaking havoc on my soul. I became angrier by the day. The tailspin had started, and I found myself struggling to stay above it. So, I do what every rational, grief-stricken person does, I go back to work. I learned quickly that it was a mistake. Three weeks went by, and I was robotic at best. When I was not working, I would go from the bed to the couch to the fridge. A devastating cycle that plummeted me further into the abyss. Unaware still of my surroundings, going through motions of muscular memory and a facade of the *'I'm ok'*. The anger boiling inside me, but the cold still sat solid in my gut, sizzling but never melting. Never leaving my soul, forever letting me feel the emptiness it released fueling the beast that emerged outwardly.

    I was so blinded by grief that I didn't even realize it was seeping over onto my family and my life. So consumed by anger and rage, I was unwittingly burning those close to me. I stopped being a wife to my husband, only going through the motions of it. Stopped taking care of myself, stopped being a mom and became a shell of the person they knew and loved. I was mean to everyone. Nasty even. No amount of apologies can ever make up for the damage my grief did. Most tragically of all, I was all those things to myself. I laid down and allowed grief to take control and allowed anger and rage to be co-pilots. I have a journal that I wrote in during this time and it is completely filled. I am terrified to read it now, to see the proof of the devastation that the death of my brother created. I know if I ever want to completely heal from it, I have to swallow that fear and read it. I let it all transform me into a wrath filled monster that does not, to this day, deserve the love my boys, my husband, my family gave to me tenfold during this time. I honestly can't tell you where I would be now if it weren't for their love helping me through it all.

I had a glimmer of hope when I learned my other brother was being released from prison, but it was soon extinguished when the realization of the fact he did not get to say goodbye to his brother, nor had he seen him the entire time he was incarcerated. This set a new precedence of grief and another layer to the cold in my gut. My heart broke all over again. I hurt more for him than I did for myself, or perhaps my hurt was just amplified by his. Either way, the tailspin continued to shove me deeper into this black hole of mourning.

I lost time, I couldn't remember if I showered one day from the next. My husband picked up the pieces and suffered greatly for it. I either didn't eat or I ate everything sometimes to the point of vomiting. I wore the same pajamas; I rarely did laundry or cleaned the house. I cooked out of obligation but did not eat with them, I did wifely duties for the same reason. I was nothing, I was walking, talking, oblivion. I took the shattered pieces of my heart and soul, and I shoved into a junk drawer, tighten the straps of my body armor and gave Anger the reins. Completely lost control of it all yet held it together so eloquently.

I wanted to escape it all, I did not want to feel this pain I was in. The euphoria after the burn never came, it burned and writhed in my veins like lava. Searing the very essence of my person. So the path of self-destruction was paved and I rode down it like a surfer on a kahuna of a wave. I did what I knew to, what I had learned to do. I survived by any means necessary. Telling myself over and over that I was *'ok, he was in a better place, and we all should be grateful.'* So, I ran. I ran from the acceptance, from the help I needed, from the family I created, I ran from myself. Searching for the anecdote. Oblivious to the fact that it laid within me. That I had the ingredients to make it.

   I ran, literally, to another state. Looking for solace and reprieve, looking for anything other than the current situation I was in. I was not only hurting from my brother's death, but there were issues my husband bequeathed to me when we married that I could no longer deal with, so I ran. Fully believing that it was not running or retreating but removing myself from it all. Removing myself from the physical would remove the metaphysical, right? Oh, how wrong I was. I was so naive to consider the notion that just because you put space and opportunity between it all, doesn't not mean it is removed, or healed, or even dealt with. But I did not care. I ran, no I fled two states away, 749 miles to be exact.

   Alone and determined to not have any more shit in my life, my house, anywhere. I left my kids, my husband, and my dogs. They soon followed, but for the first time in a long time I felt as if I could breathe. And I suppose I did for a brief moment, another glimmer of hope that 'healing' was on the horizon. It was not long before the cold awakened and gut punched me so viciously that I am still catching my breath to this day. May 14, 2018, two years, four months and fourteen days after the death of my brother, I received another bone chilling phone call from my mom telling me my nephew overdosed. Michael's beloved boy, not even 18 years old at the time, his mother came home from work that Mother's Day morning and found her son unresponsive in his bed. I know the pain of losing a child and a sibling, and my niece and sister-in-law now share that pain. Not a fate anyone should ever brag about sharing. I will forever hold her and my niece so close to my heart even more so than I ever had.

    What was left of my heart, shattered. I was at a job interview and the floor fell out from under me and I collapsed on the floor. Collecting myself I rushed out of that office and dialed my sister in law's number and begged her to tell me it was not true. Tears consumed my eyes, and it is a wonder I made the 35 miles home. Unable to drive the 749 miles back to Oklahoma, I was devastated and alone. I just sat on the couch at my best friend's house in utter shock and dismay. Luck be a son of a bitch for sure. Although you can't really group luck and death in the same basket, but damn, it sure felt like if it weren't for bad luck, we wouldn't have any. I suppose in hindsight I chose luck as an alternative to anything else. Hell, I felt I had exhausted all the others at play at this point so why not? Selfish to even think this tragedy happened to only me. No, not entirely so, we all were still hurting, still grieving the loss of my brother and you throw the loss of his son in the mix of it, it just made the wound fester and bleed even more. My heart absolutely shattered for my niece, she lost more than I or anyone else could ever lose. I can't imagine if I were to have lost my dad around the same time as my brother.

    The tailspin that had slowed ramped up again and Anger awoke Rage and we set off on an adventure of chaos and destruction. Destroying everything in its path. Leaving the rubbage to be picked up by the ones closest to me. My marriage suffered the most. The demands of his time, the constant fights about my rejection of him, the war that raged between my heart and my mind blew carnage all over the life we tried to have together. It was to a point of annihilation. So much so I contacted a divorce attorney and started making plans to leave him, to run again. Countless conversations that turned into arguments and sleepless nights. Me unable, no afraid to confront the monster of grief and despair, lashing out at his incessant clinginess and his own destructive patterns of behavior. A constant struggle of tug of a war with what I was feeling and going through and the demands of a 'good wife'.

Him not understanding what the hell was going on, thinking it was solely him and the stress he added to the situation. In part, he did not help the issue at hand, he compounded it, but it took me breaking completely for him to see through my eyes his part in the matter. It would years later that he finally understood, or began to understand, the devastation of it all. It was his love that helped to pull me back from the abyss, although I am just now able to admit that.

I struggled to maintain work, home, finances, everything. I was barely treading water and the effects of it all were beginning to show on the outside. My armor was leaking, and people were beginning to see through my facade of shit and was being called out on it. I couldn't have that. I couldn't have them coming between myself and my pain. No, it was the only thing I could feel, and I needed it, I craved it, I took it to bed and created my own beautiful paradise of hell. It was mine and no one or nothing was going to take that away from me. I felt that everything else had been ripped from me, and I would be damned if they took my pain too. How dare anyone try and help me heal, who were they to tell me anything they had no idea what I was going through much less how to help me. Right?

I think grief is the ultimate annihilator. I think once she sinks her claws into your veins, her poison slowly rolls through your veins an inch at time. Letting the burn become a part of you, slowly taking over your whole being until it is no longer blood and water in your veins. No longer you in the mirror, no longer your words, your actions, your thoughts. She gives birth to the deepest depression and the duo annihilates the very essence of you. It is a natural process, death. It is a common fate in us all, connecting us if only by that very fact.

    With death comes the grief of our loved ones who were left here to endure the process of life without you. Faring better when it was *'our time'* to go versus when they felt *'we were taken too soon.'* But is there a distinction between the two? I believe there isn't. I do not believe there is ever a right time to die, and I believe we must all be ready for it no matter the time of it. That is unpredictable. Unreasonable to even consider we could predict it. I believe grief is a selfish emotion. One birthed from jealousy. I know I felt jealous of my brother dying. I thought, *'how could he leave me here alone and why did he get to rest now?'* I was jealous that I was left here to deal with not only my demons but his. Envious that he now is free from any more pain this world could bestow upon him. Angry at the fact I was jealous of his death. Heartbroken I could never see his face again, jealous of the belief he can still see mine.

    I was vengeful, murderess even, if only in thought. I was a tornado wrapped in a hurricane and I did not care who or what I destroyed in my path. I wanted people to feel how I felt, to see and fully understand what I did. I wanted that so much that it blinded me to the chaos, pain, and destruction I was not only doing to myself, but to everyone else as well. My temper became explosive and very short fused. I demanded everything, never asking for forgiveness or offering an apology for my actions. Never cleaning up my own carnage. Forcing everyone else to eat the shit I dealt out as well as their own. I simply lost my ever-loving mind.

    So I ran again. This time to the furthest part of the map I could get, 1,236 miles to be exact. I applied to a job, I got an interview, I boarded a plane and flew solo to a place I absolutely knew nothing about to stay with someone I barely knew. Little did I know at that time, that was the best thing I could have done to heal. Up to this point, certain people could not even so much as utter my brother's name. I would shut it down real quick. I felt that certain people didn't have the right to. Their voices seemed to taint it. I would cringe at the sound his name would make when it would escape their lips. It sent shivers down my spine like nails on a chalkboard. Leaving a bitter, metallic taste in my mouth, putrid even. To this day, I have a hard time understanding why. Maybe I will never know, but what I do know is that the number of certain people has significantly dwindled recently.

    I would turn the radio off if certain songs triggered the pain. I stopped discussing the fact my brother died, I stopped responding to questions and inquiries. I kept it short and sweet, and I called it healing. I called it 'better than I was'. For all intents and purposes, maybe I was better than I was. I certainly wore a beautiful mask. I was exceptionally good at covering the scars and wounds. Proficient in the smiling face charade that portrayed a 'better Rachael'. However, those that knew me best called bullshit. It would take me another year for me to call out my own bullshit.

JOURNAL ENTRY   26 JAN 2016
' Taking time out seems impossible lately. I can't sit still, I feel like I am tweaking soberly. If I get still my mind wanders, crazy thoughts creep in, I see, I see him. I tear up when I am at work, that will not fly. I don't like questions because the ones asking usually don't have genuine or good intentions of help. I hate to cry, I don't like the feeling of hurting or weakness, BIG GIRLS DON'T CRY. I hate the red eyes and runny nose. The embarrassment of people seeing me like that and the "are you okays?' Busy, stay busy, there's no room for thoughts that make you cry when you're busy.'

2

 Maine is by far one of the most beautiful places you can ever see in the United States. I have yet to experience all the beauty of the States, but Maine is breathtaking. From her rolling hills, extravagant mountains, magnificent sunrises and sunsets, colors fit for a painter's wheel when the leaves begin to change and the picturesque snow that covers everything. To her beautiful beaches and calming waters. I have never seen something so tranquil or magnificent. The vast beauty of her definitely helped to set a broken soul at ease. I was in absolutely amazement at her beauty, but mostly at her quiet solitude and whispering trees. The wind howling through them is something out of a horror movie, and I found it eerily comforting. I found the winds to be cleansing and therapeutic. The howls taking my pain and grief and carrying them away. The midnight black skies in the winter, lit by the moon and stars that cast a blue haze over the night.
 I totally saw firsthand the hypnotic pull Maine had on people and I felt her immensely. The first I

felt the icy brick in my gut start to sweat, I was sitting in my car one dark, early morning, about to head to work. The ground was completely covered in snow and the trees bent with the weight of it. I remember thinking, *'man that tiny tree is going to break right in two from all the snow and wind.'* I just knew that if the weather kept up the way it was going it would surely be broken and laying in the yard when I returned home. I sat there a moment longer just watching it bend and creak as clumps of snow fell to the ground and more snow replaced it. Bearing all this weight and never succumbing to it. I watched it in the blue light of the moon and began to cry, unsure as to why, but I did.

  I quickly wiped my face, put my car into reverse and slowly treaded to work on the snow-covered roads. I had an hour and half ride to work and with the current conditions I had to drive slower, watching the road disappear under a cushiony, white, blanket of Maine snow. Listening as it crunched under the weight of my car. The road I stayed on was rarely, if ever, plowed. Or at least plowed last. So the two mile trek out of a valley in snow was challenging at best. Found myself in the ditch a time or two, we won't talk about that. Watching the snowfall was hypnotic in itself, good get lost in the flakes and taken away to faraway places. Reminded me of the intro to The Twilight Zone, youngins' look it up. That particular morning the air was thick with humidity and the snow fell in graceful almost angelic like waves. Once out of the valley the roads were clearer from the plow, and I relaxed a bit and eased my grip on the steering wheel. I had not realized I was squeezing it so tight until I relaxed, and my knuckles cracked from the pressure.

Still leery of the road conditions, but confident enough of the plowing, I settled in for my road trip to work. I often joke about having to pack a lunch to go to Wal-Mart in Maine and well it really wasn't a joke. Maine is notorious for its beauty and infamous for its ruralness. The snow continued to fall, and I drifted back to the tree. The tall, thin tree and the weight it was carrying, and I began to cry again. This time I couldn't stop. I cried the entire way to work. I was dumbfounded as to why I had suddenly become a blubbering idiot on my way to work. Over a tree. Looking at it now, it wasn't the tree, it was me and all the weight I was carrying, bending and creaking against it, getting some reprieve when snow would fall off only to have fresh piled on. At that time, I did not know, or perhaps I didn't want to know why.

My health started to fail prior to my adventure to Maine, and in Maine it all but tanked and after seeing countless doctors, I made a decision that I needed to start taking care of myself better and that needed to start with my mental health. Crying over a tree was, in my book, an indication I was spent mentally and emotionally. We all know how stress can take its toll on a person, add grief and physical ailment to the pot, and well, you have yourself a shit stew of a life. Doesn't sit well with the pallet and I have yet to find a wine that would complement it.

I was attending church at my in-law's church, my father in-law the local pastor there. At first it was nice to get to hear his sermons and see into his life as a pastor. I grew up in the church, literally. My maternal grandfather was a preacher as well as my paternal grandmother. I never felt right sitting in pews, never understanding why. Never comprehending the semantics of it but enjoyed the camaraderie and the community of it. So sitting in a pew next to my mother in-law, felt nice. However, sitting there would be the most I would ever do. I tried to get involved in it, I tried to become this *'good Christian daughter in-law'*, but soon felt the weight of obligation and I did not want that, I needed something else. I needed to heal, and I was not getting that in those pews.

I absolutely love my in-laws. I do not know any other woman that can honestly say she adores her mother-in-law, but I do. I don't have to agree with them in order to love them. I felt I could talk to her; felt she listened and did not judge. She did help me to shed some light on why I was so angry, on why I was so sick, despite God being shoved down my throat, she helped me see past that and let me make up my own mind. That is why I love her so. My husband has told me they were raised the same way. To make up their own minds on the direction of their faith. Odd commodity to me, as I grew up way different than that. I grew up being told that unless I turned it all over to God, got in bed with God, did everything according to God, God, God, then my life would always be crap. That I would never heal, and all my problems were because I turned away from God. Who ever said I did?

I would come to choke on the very word. Hated it being forced fed. I am a believer in a higher power. I do know that there is something or someone out there that is bigger than I could ever be, greater, wiser. I also believe that it is my free will to believe that I am also my own maker. Without the two coming together, one will not work without the other. Sitting in the pews with my mother-in-law, I was reminded of the suffocating feeling of being force fed religion. I realized that I felt better in nature. I have always loved being outside. Barefoot in the grass feeling the Earth's vibrations seep in through the soles of my feet. Invigorating my soul, constantly reminded that we came from her and we will return to her. And for all you God fearing people, what better way to serve and honor him than being in the midst of all that he created.

I found that sitting alone in the early mornings, drinking coffee, listening to their clock tick, tears would flow and my mind would drift back to that January night, and I would watch as tears dripped into my coffee. Each tear drop shedding the weight I had been carrying of that night. Not understanding at that moment, that it was not just the grief that would leak through my eyes, but trauma, pain, loss, abuse, all of the weight would release through tears. Each one a snowflake, different from the last.

Writing has always been a way that I could just dump my brain so I could regroup and refocus. So I started doing that very thing. On the mornings of my tear coffee creamer, I would take my phone, open the notes section of it and just type. Before I knew it I had several pages filled and cold cups of coffee. I slowly felt that ice brick in my gut start to melt. I have been alone most of my life, but I have never sat alone with my only company being myself. To sit with yourself, really get into your brain and walk around in it, is not for the faint of heart. The strongest warriors are brought to their knees at the confrontation of themselves. So writing, although easy to do, was rather difficult, brutal, and messy.

I wrote not with the intention of dealing with anything, but so that I could clear my brain of clutter, adjust my armor and tread on. I was ignorantly unaware of the benefit it was bestowing on me. The loss of my brother was embedded deep, intertwined with my soul. Writing seemed to help loosen its grip. The longer I would sit with myself, the tighter the grip, the more I wrote while sitting with myself, the looser it became. It was excruciating, and I found myself struggling to breathe even more so. The constant fluctuation between pain and comfort deeply bruised my intentions. I wanted to stop, I didn't want to hurt anymore as I had become so immune to the pain and grief that the release, no matter how minute, stung and ached something fierce. I didn't know then that the hurt I was feeling, I needed it. The offensiveness of it was justifiable brutality.

My husband suggested that we take up hiking in the backwoods of Maine. A venture that I excitedly welcomed. One spring day when we thought the snow had melted enough, we packed a backpack, donned our hiking boots and headed out to see where the forest would take us. It wasn't long before we were ankle deep in snow, but we didn't care. We trekked on until the only sounds we could hear aside from our breathing was the forest. I stopped and closed my eyes and listened to the voices of the trees, the whispers of the wind, and in my tranquility, I heard my brother's voice. I heard him say, *'listen.'* and I did just that, I listened. Desperate to hear him again, I listened.

I listened to the ice brick in my gut melt some more, I listened to the wind caress my pain and strip it away with each stroke. I listened to the forest as she wrapped her arms around me and held me tight, whispering to me to let it all go. The stubbornness of that which is me, shook out of her grasp and moved fervently through the forest next to my husband, only reveling in her beauty and ignoring her healing. Unwillingly, I emerged from the hike feeling refreshed and more energized, but I justified it as the exercise we obtained from the hike.

We would seek out trails and mountains and beaches to hike. Each time I would feel better and better, but again exercise, right? I have no doubt the exercise helps in recovery, healing, and transformations. I just was not able to discern between those notions at the time. What was healing? What were transformations? What was anything other than the suffering I had known for so long? I was convinced that this was just how it was going to be, and if I could get healthier then that was enough. That was going to be the magic that it took to be free of pain.

My favorite place to be is the beach. I was 34 years old the very first time I saw the ocean. My husband took me to Mississippi the March after our wedding for a late honeymoon and I fell in love with her right then and there. Lost in the cadence of her waves and the soothing voice as they crashed to shore. The smell of salt invigorating my senses. So it only made sense that we seek her out anyway we could. Maine has some of the most beautiful beaches, even those that are rocky, and some of the clearest fresh waters I have ever seen. Reflective even in cloudy skies. Just breathtakingly beautiful. The rivers and lakes are vibrant and alive, the ocean very vocal and calm at the same time. It is no wonder people flock to Maine in the summer months.

I found quiet and solitude on any of her banks, my favorite being the little coves my husband and I would seek out. No tourists, barely even locals, just us and the water. We found a little cove one warm spring day and we sat on some boulders in a front row seat for beauty. The tide was slowly creeping in and we sat watching it slither in. I found myself talking to it. Asking it how she could go away like that to return changed and more alive than ever. Asking her how she could go through something so traumatic to come back more beautiful and stronger than ever.

    She answered me with the crashing of the waves against the shore, each one vibrational and electrifying. The sound of the water hypnotizing the pain, easing it into submission and coaxing it for release. I never wanted to leave the beach, never wanted to be without her addicting voice. I started to hear the waves in my sleep, a soothing lullaby that allowed me to drift off into the blue light of night. The dreams came more frequently of him, more confusing yet comprehensible. I would hear his voice telling me to listen, I would wake to him calling my name. The dreams were not of what was him, but of what he was now. Forever the protector, forever the big brother.

    They made me think that maybe he was hurting too, and that he could not rest because I was not at peace. He came to me every night in my dreams, so vivid, so real. Sometimes not saying a word, just sitting with me until I woke. I often woke up to tears soaking my pillow. Trying desperately to go back to sleep to see him one more time, angry at the morning light of reality. An incredible cycle that repeated every day until I understood exactly what it was, I needed to do.

I needed to let the anger and rage go, but I was afraid. I was afraid to give up that control, afraid that if I let it go, then the world would see the pain it covered and the shame it masked. Afraid to allow anyone to see me exposed and bare. If I let go of anger and rage then I had nothing to shield the pain and anguish and I would be forced to deal with it. Forced to remove that too. The only way I felt that I could do this was to have help, but who? Who could possibly understand what it was I needed to do and have the resources to help me do it? A counselor, a stranger I didn't know. My husband, who could not even begin to imagine the pain I suffered, the trauma, the heartbreak?

'Take me to the beach', I would tell him, and he would with love and adoration. Never complaining how many times I asked, or how long we would stay. He would notice when I would walk away, and he would stay behind. I never questioned him on this, I suppose I knew the reason. I needed my alone time with the water. I needed the therapy she provided to me. I needed to lose myself in the rhythmic white noise of her waves against the shore. To hear her, to feel her power wash away the anger and rage so that I could sit with the pain, feel it, understand it, and learn how to let it all go.

3

Losing a loved one is never easy. Doesn't matter who it is. It places a vice around your heart and squeezes. Eventually we either learn to live it or we find a way to loosen its grip. The pain I felt when my brother died was none like I have ever felt before, compounded by the tumultuous life I lived and the stress I was under. The vice grip locked and rusted around my heart. One of the only people who could 'save me' from myself was gone. What could I do now but exist? I was doing that very thing extremely well. Going through the motions of every day. Slowly drowning. What better way to deal with it all than getting lost in water?

Memories flood your brain, like an invasion of ants, crawling over everything. Consuming anything in their path. No matter how much you try you just can't seem to separate them from anything else. Water seems to be the only thing that could disrupt their destructive invasion. Clearing them out so you can see what exactly it is that has a hold of their attention and rid of its contents. The problem is you can't just stick a garden hose up your nose and hope for the best no and I wouldn't recommend trying that approach either.

    Getting lost in the tantalizing rhythm of waves is a better approach to flooding your nostrils with tap water. The pull of the moon to direct the flow, working in unison of the stages of the night to bring forth anything and everything that needs cleansing, including grief. For my 40th birthday I was supposed to take a cruise, but the pandemic saw to it that it was not in the cards to do so, so I settled for three nights on the beach. Just me, the cool crisp salty air and the water. My birthday falls in late September, so the air was not quite warm but not quite freezing either. I would say it was perfect.

By now I had survived 4 years without my brother and that is an understatement on just how well I had been doing up to this point. I was anything but ok, and the year I had spent in Maine so far was bringing it all to the surface. Not just his death, but everything. Every hurt, pain, traumatic experience everything! I noticed the effect dealing with myself had on me when I was able to host my mom for the summer prior to my birthday. The sheer fact she lasted a month with me is growth in and of itself. I had not yet forgiven her for what she had done, but I had taken responsibility for my part. I know people say that abuse and trauma is never the victim's fault, this is very true. But my reaction to it, my hatred, my anger, was just that, mine. I alone control nothing but myself. I can't control things that are done to me, but I can control how I respond to them. So, the growth I noticed in having her spend that month with me told me just how much time I wasted in my head.

So, for my 40th, I booked a hotel for three days about 200 feet from the shoreline. I opened the balcony doors and let the crashing of the waves sing their lullaby to me as I contemplated my next move. I knew I was hurting; I could feel it. I knew I had to stop because it was literally killing me. I just didn't know where to begin. Unaware that the work had already begun. There was an extra blanket in the closet of the hotel, so I took it with my beach blanket, and I headed down with my husband to the beach. The air was chilly but not overtly so. I picked a spot that sat in the setting sun and settled in to count my blessings that I made it another year.

As we watched the water, I started to feel the ache inside me come to the surface and struggle to get free. I didn't want to let it go. I wanted to hold onto it, wanted to shove it down into the abyss never to let it see the light of day. I was even more afraid than ever. Afraid that if I let it go, even just a little, I would indeed lose him completely as well. I was holding on to the notion that if I just stayed angry, stayed hurt, traumatized, that I could stay his sister. Not fully knowing that I would always be his sister and he my brother regardless if he were here in the flesh or not. I couldn't bear the thought of him fading into the abyss as well. Forgetting his face, his laughter, the sound of his voice.

The universe telling me it was ok was not good enough. I needed assurance, I needed tangible proof of that notion. I was not going to just accept it as true. My stubbornness and my incessant need for proof is a toxicity so fowl that the acceptance of that as well as the ownership of it, burned like pure grain alcohol on the back of my throat. Giving even the smallest inch could be fatal. At least that's what my survival brain told my heart. I have lived in complete and utter survival. Not living at all. Taking every hit to my heart, to my conscience, like a tank in battle. I had to, I had to be strong, I couldn't show weakness. I had people watching me, depending on me.

These thoughts ran rampant in my brain as the waves rolled in and out against the white capped shore. The sun setting and illuminating the sand and water in a purple hue, dancing on the water. My husband sat next to me and covered my shoulders with the extra blanket as the evening chilled the air even more. He never said a word to me. I loved that about him, He just lets me be and lets me talk when I am ready. Maybe he knew what was running through my mind, maybe he didn't. Either way he just sat with me and watched the water.

Each sway of the tide took me deeper into myself. I felt the claws of the hurt scraping my throat as tears swelled into my eyes. I just watched the water. I never took my eyes off of its glorious movement. Against all fibers of my being, I let the tears burn my cheeks and kiss my lips. I whispered, *'You should be here.'* I closed my eyes to listen. I let the hypnotic roll of the waves flood my ears and carry me away. I let the flow take me to the hurt to the pain and I let the ebb take them away.

Healing from tragedy is rough, but healing from a lifetime of tragedy compounded with grief, is brutal and heinous. Hurting more to let it go, cauterizing the festered wounds, leaving beautifully placed scars. Never forgetting the pain, but no longer feeling it or living it. I have only just begun to heal, not quite to the scarred phase entirely. Not knowing which wound to tend to first, I decided to tend to the most recent and allow for that healing to take place.

I made, no I accepted, a decision to let go of anger and rage that September day on the beach. I decided to allow grief her proper place in the succession and accept her as priority. I did not realize until that night that I had not grieved. Truly grieved for my brother's passing. I had not even allowed the consideration. I spent years just angry, out of control, lost and sullen, that I did not grasp the gravity of the passing of my beloved brother. I was not honoring him. I was being selfish and ridiculous.

Forgiving others is easier than forgiving yourself. Acknowledging that you are in need of forgiveness from others is even easier than acknowledging it to yourself in the mirror. My brother would not have wanted me to carry on in the way I had been. He would say *'Rach, you of all people should not be doing this!'* Hell, he said it enough to me when he was alive, and well he would be right every single time. Never apologetic for calling anyone out on their shit, especially his sister.

The three days I spent on that beach, profoundly ground in just how heavy the ice brick was in my gut. Just how frostbitten I truly had become and how I was going to thaw from it all. I never truly accepted the fact that he was gone, I never truly accepted the trauma I experienced in my life so that notion makes sense that I would follow suit with the death of my brother. I was lost to my own device and the weight of it all was more than my armor could withstand.

Spending a year and a half in solitude, having the means to sit with myself as well as the courage, helped shed terrific light on everything that was dark in my life. The darkest being my brother's death. For the first time I started to breathe. I was still a stranger to one in the mirror, but I could breathe easier. I started to re-evaluate my life and my situations and began to make sense of it all. Tracing every wound, every scar, every hurt, with softer fingers. Really feeling each one gingerly with a new curiosity to really know them.

My whole world shattered under those blue lights that New Year's night, and every New Year's Eve when my husband and I celebrate another matrimonious year; I am constantly reminded that an amazing night ended with the tragedy of a new year. I could not celebrate the years with my wonderful husband, because I felt if I showed even an ounce of happiness, my brother would be forgotten. How selfish was I? How self-absorbed to think that my happiness could ever replace him?

Selfish to even consider anything above my own anger and pain. Letting go of all that, I was finally able to allow the tears to flow for my brother, for the life we had together, for the life he lived and for the mark he left on this world, on me. Living in Maine, as far away from anything that reminded me of him except myself. Trying to escape my own skin was futile, but damn it I tried. I tried to run as far and as fast as I could even though I was right on my own heels.

Grief settled in and she loosened the grip around my heart. She allowed the pain to well up in my eyes, get heavy and fall. She assured me that every time it would hurt, but when it was done there would be a masterpiece left where chaos resided. I was reminded that even though I was in control, I had to submit to her every time. The dreams kept coming, more of him just sitting with me in a room to ourselves. His million-dollar smile reflected in his eyes. Some, where he would talk to me, tell me that everything will be ok. Others he would show me glimpses of things I buried. My own personal guide to the blue light nights of my past.

JOURNAL ENTRY   28 JAN 2016

' had a rough morning driving to work. Songs making me think, cry. I hate crying. I heard his voice saying,' suck it up Barnes, we don't cry.' I turned on some heavy metal and rocked out. It has been getting easier, I think, maybe, hell I don't know. I've to stay busy, too busy it seems. Keep my thoughts random. My head is full of things to do next. I feel overwhelmed and anxious when I get still, even at bedtime it is hard to sleep. Mom makes it difficult to cope. With her meddling and incessant schemes. God, please help her. I want to believe her intentions are good, but when is enough, enough. I know what it is like to lose a child, the pain is unbearable, never goes away… Mike is and will always be a big part of me, there isn't a memory good or bad that he isn't in. I feel lost and disconnected. I hate how she can't see that. God, please help her.'

4

The very thought of not seeing my brother is still a hard pill to swallow to this day. I don't think there will ever be enough water to get it down without it stinging and scraping my throat and hitting my stomach like a ton of bricks. Every time my mother says his name, I still tighten my lips and tense up. I stopped talking to her, literally, for 6 months after my brother died. I was infuriated at her demeanor, her actions, her very essence, during that time. I was angry that I was completely blinded to her pain. I could have cared less. I was glad she was hurting, and I wanted her to suffer for it all.

I wanted her to feel every sting of it. I was satisfied when I didn't answer her calls or accept her pleas to other family members on her behalf. I wanted no part in it at all. I hoped that she was finally seeing the damage she caused and what it led to. I was amazed at the effort she put into trying to force her way back into my life. Overstepping boundaries. After 6 months I think I was just too numb to even care anymore, and I allowed her to come into my home only to have regretted that decision almost immediately. I was constantly shutting her down when she would talk about my brother, my dad, or anything I felt she didn't have a right to talk about. This led to her angrily leaving my house and another sporadic, even more volatile relationship with me. I didn't hate her, no, I was pissed at why she didn't try this damn hard from the beginning. I thought maybe, just maybe if she did, my brother would not be laying six feet deep in a cold, lonely grave.

    Distance was not enough, she would always over do, over speak, over share anything going on with me. I felt violated and it just fueled my anger and rage even more. I blocked her completely from everything. Phone, social media, I stopped including her in my life, in my kids' life. Everything. The funny thing about that is, I didn't have to. She was never really a part of any of that, and my anger just sealed the deal even more so. I could not deal with the fact that she could not take responsibility for her part in it all. So consumed with that, I couldn't even take responsibility for my own shit.

    Moving to Maine allowed, no, forced me to do that very thing. Forced me to recognize that anger and rage fueled hate and animosity and that gave birth to a vengeful appetite. An appetite so ravenous that it was never satisfied, and I consumed detrimentally. Slowly poisoning that which was me.

We all grieve in different ways, we all cope, deal, struggle, according to our own mind set. Some of us freak out, some withdrawal, some of us never deal at all. I think I am some of it all, that what I thought was healing and coping was really an illusion.

It wasn't until I sat across from her at my in-laws' table and I saw defeat on her face, that I knew the damage that had been done was done, and I was ashamed. I have never been an eye for an eye kind of person, or at least I fooled myself into believing that. And that was exactly what I had done to her. For all her faults, she did not deserve my wrath. If for the very least, the satisfaction of bringing me to her level. She deserved to grieve and heal and I was not the person to tell her she couldn't. In that epiphanic moment, I grew and healed a little more. The sting and taste of it is still fresh on my heart and tongue.

I have never not loved my mom or respected her, I was angry, hurt, and confused. I never could and still can't wrap my brain around why anyone would treat their children, their daughter the way I was. But it was not for me to understand, for I never could. It was for me to become better than that, to rise above it all and to make sure I broke the cycle. I did that by not raising my boys the same as I and I continue to do it by grieving the loss of childhood, my brother, and healing from it all.

The only thing I regret is the fact my brother had to die for me to see this. For me to actually deal with it all and heal. I noticed the fact that it took his death for my mom to realize whatever demon in herself to make changes, but I was too damn blinded by my own to do the same. It was almost like the glue started to peel in our family. My dad calls more, my other brother said, *'I love you Rach,'* more, and my own boys are closer. In a desperate attempt to hold what was left tightly together. So, what the hell was wrong with me? Me, always on the outside waiting to get in. So used to the cold, heat feels wrong.

    Being in Maine helped me to appreciate the cold. Not only literally with her brutal winters, but figuratively as well. When you are snowed in for days at a time you get creative, or you get cabin fever, and I did both. Creatively curing cabin fever was no easy feat, especially when left to your own devices and demons. I learned to accept what was and let go of what I could. Some things are forever embedded into you that letting go is not an option, so you get creative and adapt. We as humans are an incredible species and have perfected the ability to adapt to our ever-changing surroundings. I felt I was the one human who struggled with this. I thought I was the only one feeling this much pain, and that no one else could ever help, understand, much less possibly fathom what I went through and am going through. Adapting taught me I was wrong. It forced me to change how I spoke, how I reacted, how I grew and healed. I don't think I could have done this very thing had my actions not led me to a rural valley in Maine.

I remember the moment I let grief completely tear my soul apart and cleanse me of my hurt and pain for Michael. I was sitting once again in my car this time after work, and I was mesmerized by the full moon gallantly staring back at me. The most beautiful aspect of Maine to me is how close the sky is. Like I am on the top rung of the ladder to the heavens and all I have to do is stretch my arm out to touch it. This night the moon was so big, so bright that it lit the inside of my car and the surrounding area on the darkest street. I love all things moon related. I am truly in awe of his magnificent power. This night he was encased in clouds, but his magnitude towered over them.

I watched in pure astonishment, just transfixed on him and my eyes began to sting as I once again said, *"you should be here."* I thought I heard him say, *'I am'*, and a white-hot pain seared through my soul and erupted out of my body and flooded my cheeks. I did not try to stop it, I couldn't. I let grief take over and I let her tear it all down as I watched the moon through clouded eyes. I have no idea how long I sat in that car that night, but I didn't care. I needed the offensiveness of it. I have only ever learned the hard way, and grief knew that. She knew the only way to feel better is to cut it deeper. To go below the festered wounds and peel it away a layer at time. It is the only way to allow healing, to allow growth.

I look at the moon through different eyes now. My love for it runs deeper than ever before. I felt his collusion with grief that night so profoundly and understood their attack on my pain was strategic and well executed, pure and deserved. As much as I did not like it, it needed to happen. I was drowning in my own shit that was affecting my health, my home, my marriage. A cancer so out of control that it would take a miracle to cure, and I believe that night in my car with that massive full moon, I touched the very beginning of a miracle.

It only took one time to have me wanting that feeling of release. The electrifying sensation that coursed through my body, the feeling of being able to take a breath and not feel the pain so much, was more than enough to make me want to shed more, to heal more, to grow more. It was an epic realization of just how much pain I was in. I had let the cold settle and let it mask it all. I let it make me a zombie, a mindless, heartless, shell of a person. With that realization had to come acceptance and ownership. There wasn't any way around it.

I had to accept that he was gone, I had to own that I could not call him up just for shits and giggles. I had to accept that letting him go does not mean he is gone, it meant that I could go one without him and I would be ok. That everything he was to me, he still is. Everything he taught me I still knew and that everything from this point on, he has influenced. I was not honoring him; I was burying him. It was time to honor him and allow that hurt to heal so that I could start another cycle of grief, letting go, healing and growing. I had to own up to the hurt I caused in the wake of anger's destruction and make amends not only to those that I hurt, but more importantly to myself. My dad once told me, *'Baby girl, doing things for yourself is not selfish, it's self-care.'* I had to own that.

Healing is ugly, it is not rainbows and kittens, it is brimstone and fire. It is necessary in order to not fall into a bottomless pit and be suspended in nothingness. Healing from loss is even more so. The devastation I felt, I have no words to describe. I lost a child of my own and that did not strike me as hard as the loss of my brother. Maybe the combination of the two was just more than I could have imagined. Maybe it was because my baby was still born, where I had a lifetime with my brother. Whatever the reason, if there is one, left a wound so raw and exposed in my soul.

They say time heals all wounds; I say they are wrong. Time does not heal anything; it puts a band aid on it. It allows for the ability to shove it all down and keep moving forward, because that's what we do. I believe that 'in time' we either learn to deal with it or we learn to live with it, neither way heals. Healing needs to be grotesque and consistent. Like changing bandages every day from a bullet wound. Cleaning out the festering part, placing new bandages on it. Each time it heals more, each time it makes an atmosphere for a beautifully placed scar to form and one hell of a story to tell.

I know what stress and turmoil can do to a person, I never thought it would ever tear me down the way it did. I thought I could handle anything. I had survived some of the most vicious and unimaginable things and was even more sure I could handle the death of my brother. I was wrong in all the ways you can imagine. I mean, I handled his death in the same way I handled the trauma and other stress in my life. I sucked it all in, pulled my big girl panties up and I never let any of them see me cry. I never let anyone get too close afraid they would see the wounds, or worse smell the rot that had set in. Healing stepped in and said *hold my beer I bet I could shake some shit up.*

There is never a good time to heal, it is a necessity and will force its hand if need be. It is not something you prepare for. I have heard others tell me that *'when you're ready Rachael, you will.'* I was never ready. Pain is addictive. Healing means there won't be any more pain, right? Or that's what I thought. I found that healing doesn't take away the pain. The hurt I feel, I still feel to this day, it has been 7.5 years and there is still an ache in my heart. A memory of the ice brick that laid heavily in my gut. Healing allows me to write these words, although difficult, without pause or tear stained eyes. To talk about him with ease. To honor him as he should be honored and remembered. It has also allowed me to be more open about the other past traumas I endured in my lifetime.

I was not ready to allow anyone to see that side of me, not ready to see myself raw and exposed in the mirror. Some never heal, some fall victim to the addiction of the pain. I allowed my pain to be touched, to be comforted, to be bandaged and cleansed over and over again. It allowed me to feel more than the pain and the hurt. I gained a better respect for myself, for my brother, for all the blue light nights of my past and present. Tragedy happens, stress happens, I was not ready for a new way to handle those things when they do. Healing showed me a way.

My best friend sat in my car with me a few weeks ago, and just listened to my mouth ramble out what my brain wanted to say. I have always been the advice giver and never the taker. I have listened to those that have spewed their thoughts and opinions, rarely taking heed to what they had to say. Too damn stubborn to even consider it. That night, we sat in my car in her driveway and I, for the first time in the 24 years we have been friends, opened a door and let her see into that room of my psyche. She later told me that she was shocked and appreciative that I trusted her enough to tell her the things that I told her.

I never not trusted her. I didn't trust myself. I was comfortable telling her or anyone some of the things that I needed to say. Unsure as to why I was so afraid, I just was. I am still afraid, afraid that what I have to say will deter those I am opening up to, away from me. Afraid that my damaged and broken person will be too much for anyone to handle. I am learning this is a response to the trauma and not an actual occurrence. My dad tells me all the time,' *those that stay, stay, no matter what.'* I finally understood that that statement goes for me too.

Healing did not and has not prepared me for any of it. I learn as I go. There are moments where I still need to be left alone. I prefer it, and that's ok. I get overstimulated and I need the time to regroup and refocus. The difference is, when I have had my moment, I can sit down with my husband, my friend, or even you the reader, and allow you all to see behind the door I needed time to open.

The brother door was the hardest to open and even harder to close. I don't think I will ever completely close it, only time will. It still stings and burns a little where the frostbite took its toll. I respect the colder months more than I have ever before. It's amazing how certain events put a brand on your heart, how certain smells and sounds take you back. When Michael died, I stopped letting those things take me back. I stopped reveling in the nostalgia of it. I would scroll past pictures of him, turn off music that reminded me of him, stopped cooking things he liked to eat, stopped even mentioning his name.

That was not healing or handling any damn thing, I was blinded by the ever-present survival of my life. I was numb to it all until that faith filled, full moon night when I was brought to my knees. Healing is brutal and rightfully so, and I think that is why we think we have to prepare for it. And why some of us never really heal from these things. Or at least that is my belief of the matter. I know I didn't and honestly, I can say that had I not succumbed to it, I probably would not be here writing this.

I have always wondered why I was even still here, wondered why there was not a second plot next to my brother's. I may never know the exact answer and it very well could be a rhetorical thought. I do know that looking back on everything it was my "I will show you,' attitude. My ridiculous obsession with proving people wrong. My outright stubbornness to be more than what everyone deemed me to be. I was super focused on making sure others knew I was just fine and doing everything they said I couldn't, that I failed to see the destruction I had created along the way. The song lyrics by Billie Joel, *'only the good die young,'* took on a whole new meaning when my brother died. He was 5 months shy of his 40th birthday. Although I am willing and ready to meet my maker when my time comes, I couldn't miss the subliminal message of those words.

I haven't been good, not by a longshot. Being a good person, always doing what is right, taking care of what needs to be taken care of, does not mean that I was 'good'. The anger, the hate, the pain, everything that is harsh to the tongue when spoken, I was wrapped up in. Slowly poisoning myself and everything in my path. Healing showed me the trail of casualties in my wake. A very hard image to see, an even harder reconciliation.

It showed me how I can go back and repair what I can and rebuild what I can't. It also showed me where I tried to repair and rebuild what I did not break and helped me to understand that I had to forgive myself for trying. The hardest of those was the death of my brother. That I had to let him go and let his maker do the repairs and rebuild, and that in his place I could do something, I could plant something new, something admirable and honorable to myself and to him. I read a quote by Audi Brown that says,`` *You are responsible for how long you let what hurt you, haunt you."* I spent, no I wasted years not taking this responsibility. Not reconciling things that needed it and not putting others to bed that didn't.

JOURNAL ENTRY   30 JAN 2016
'...mind just wanders and I want to do is sleep, but at night I see him. God help to fade this from my sight. I know I can't erase it, but please can you help me to fade it enough so I can sleep'... 'I see myself getting angry quickly and not wanting to be around my boys or my husband. I feel consumed, claustrophobic, and restless'...

5

I hate the phrase, *'oh you'll get over it!'* Like damn Karen, have a heart much. I remember after my brother's funeral, my dad attended the funeral of one of his family members and his sister, the mother of the cousin who was with my brother that night, saw my dad. He, being just as stubborn and it's where I get it from, kept his distance from her. Whether rightfully so or not, the death of my brother was still very raw at this time and my dad was very hurt and angry. She walks up to him and yells,*' he's dead, get over it!'* Now I was not there to witness this, however, several people heard her say this to my dad.

I will never forget the look on his face as he was telling me this story. I have never, I mean never, seen this man cry much less break down in pure agony, at his own sister talking to him like that. I went back to my conversation with my brother where I told him I never wanted to see him again and I lost it. I had to leave my dad's place and I drove the hour and half back to my house in silence. I told my husband about the conversation my dad had, and I remember saying to him,*' can you imagine saying something like that to your sister or brother?'* Big ass, spiked, pill I just swallowed right there.

These things you don't just reach into your head, fumble around in the dark until you find the switch and turn it off. Not how this works, believe me I tried. Never found that damn switch. What I did find was far more illuminating than any light could be, but that was after I sat in the cold dark. Looking back at all this, it was a wonder that I did not get lost in the thick of it. Perhaps I did for a time, pretending that I knew what I was doing and where I was going. Wandering around aimlessly in a poetic posture, giving the illusion I had my shit together. The fact being, I was only fooling myself. I was only putting on a show in my mind while the rest of the world saw a disastrous train wreck.

We can't take back words, but we can correct actions. I spent way too much time on the words I said to Michael just two months before his death, not wanting to accept the fact that his actions at my wedding corrected the actions of his sister. I was way too damn angry, I had to let that go before I realized that all was forgiven in that instance. I still have a hard time to this day. His birthday passed recently, and I felt off all day, but I did not cry nor was I angry. Just a little unsettled. That, my friend, is healing. Two years ago in Maine, I decided I wanted to do something for him and honor him on his 44th birthday. I bought 44 balloons and I had my husband drive me out to Marsh Point lighthouse in Maine. A beautiful lighthouse on a rocky shoreline of Maine. I had seen a picture of it and was drawn to its mysterious beauty and an electrifying feeling flooded my veins and I knew this was the place to let him go.

I took those 44 balloons and I walked alone down the long pier that ended at the lighthouse. I stood on the right of the door and looked out at the semi calm water. The wind was brisk that day causing small waves to lap over the rocks of the shore. A beautiful blue sky, fluffy clouds and a warming sun. I turned my tear-soaked face to the sun and closed my eyes. I whispered, *'you should be here, but I have to let you go. Until I see you again, I love you.'* The wind picked up and blew the balloons around my body. I smiled as I let them go. I stood there watching them float magnificently away. They lingered a moment almost as if he turned to wave at me and then soared towards the heavens. I felt this shift in my person and a shock wave roared through me, and I knew. I knew that I would never 'get over' his death, but that I could heal and have a life after his death.

I said earlier that time does not heal, time does allow for the space and opportunity to heal. I felt I was stuck in a time loop. Just repeating the day over and over again. The memories of that plagued my nights and infiltrated my days. I could not sleep and if I weren't occupied during the day, I climbed the walls. I had no clue this was not how grief works, all I knew was, if I'm busy I don't think and if I don't think I won't hurt and that's healing right? Apparently, my life up to this point says that is a lie.

I couldn't just work it away. I couldn't stay occupied enough to even try. The sleepless nights were definitely taking its toll on me, and I was suffering more in the day from it. Something had to give and give it did.

I said previously that healing was a bitch to be reckoned with and boy I thought I had her whipped. I couldn't have been more wrong. I am still transitioning, still healing and still hurting at the same time. It is a process, and it will take time, however, I no longer fight the lessons it is trying to teach me. I have a lot I need healing from, not just the death of my brother. I just prioritized the areas I needed to heal from starting with what I felt was the worst of them all.

Michael David Barnes was born May 24, 1976, to a fifteen-year-old mother and an eighteen-year-old father. Babies themselves. His middle name is my dad's first name and if that isn't an indication, he was loved by them, I don't know what is. My mother was a very young and troubled mother and despite it all, I believe she tried as did my dad. Looking back at photographs of my brother as a baby he was a happy baby, or it seemed. I began to see his smile fade with each picture as his demons settled in. We will never know the pain his demons caused, but I felt it all, the day he died. I felt them scream in agony from my own lips. I felt them searching for their vessel that laid on the floor of that house. I heard their anguish as his maker took him home. I felt his pain leave his body and his soul rested.

The only comfort I took during that time was the fact that he was no longer feeling any more pain. That comfort has helped me get to where I am today. Almost a decade later, allowing you the reader a glimpse into my horrific healing from one of the most tragic blue light nights in my life. It is ironic that I lost my daughter in the middle of the night, my brother, and my grandfather. It was not until right now as I am typing this that I realized, damn what a way to go, in the presence of the ultimate light to guide them into their next life. The Moon.

He was charismatic, funny, and intelligent. He never backed down from anything; he always spoke his mind. He taught me to never be afraid of anything or anyone, including myself. He was a dedicated father and loved his wife and kids more than he loved himself. I hope they knew that, despite it all, I hope they do. He was my biggest fan and even harder critic. I always wanted his opinion and advice. I still seek it to this day. I still look to the heavens and ask him to hold my hand as I step off any cliff. He did not deserve any of this but I am sure glad he lived the life he did. I am so blessed to have known him in any context.

The circumstances of his death are suspicious at best. The coroner ruled that he died from an aortic aneurysm. Basically, the main vein of his heart exploded. He was dead before he even knew it. The 'overdose' theory was squashed with this revelation, however, the events of that night lead us all to believe that there is far more to this story. My relentless brain and my incessant need to know why has me to this day questioning everything. I am only saddened by the fact that he was treated poorly. He deserves to have justice. I know that his cause of death was basically 'natural causes,' but what about the manner? Where did the bruises come from the funeral director found or the suspicious behavior of my cousin? There are people that know the truth and that is all we as his family want.

   No, we will never 'get over it.' Not with so many unanswered questions, but for me at least I now can process this in a better light, in a better mind frame. One free of the anger and the rage that consumed my life for so long. I can now sleep better at night. I now allow his name to be spoken by those I previously deemed unworthy to even think they could. I would not be able to do any of this had I not gone inside my head and pulled Rachael out. I am ok with letting my husband in to see the damage this has caused me and allow him to touch the most vulnerable places I had tucked away.

   I didn't realize that I welcomed Michael's demons to take up residence with my own until I released them. That electric sensation I felt that May afternoon on that pier was grief opening their cages and letting them free. Am I still grieving? Some. The tears on my computer as I write this are proof. Am I better than I was? No doubt. I will never forget when the moon and my grief colluded to attack my senses and beautifully forced me to let go. I have seen people hold on to such things and have seen the effects it has done to them, but I couldn't see mine. Not before that cold, full moon night in Maine.

The hardest thing a parent will ever do, but should never have to do, is bury a child. It is the most excruciating pain one can ever feel. The pain of losing my brother is tied with that. I am a rare breed and have the unfortunate reality of knowing what it feels like to lose both. I am getting better with every day. Time makes it easier, but not better. That is something I have to work at every single day. The sting of it lessens every day. I am now able to celebrate my anniversary with my amazing husband without anxiety, dread, or over sensitivity. I can now face each New Year's Day with honor and grace.

I no longer seek a New Year's resolution; no, I seek revolutions. I seek constitutional empowerment. I tackle a new pain every year. Yes, I said year. Each one needs its own time to grieve, time to heal and time to let go. Each year I get closer to a completely new Rachael. One that never forgets but lives and forgives. Forgives herself mainly and foremost. I cannot forgive others, if I cannot forgive myself for the damage I have allowed or caused. Forgiveness needs to be first inward before it can be outward. That too was difficult to swallow. The cold that set in 7 years ago, I can still feel, but it is felt only as a memory. One where I control the response or attention, I give it.

Michael David Barnes died January 1, 2016, on a frigid Oklahoma night. He was with people he thought he trusted. His guard was down as he allowed his baby cousin to fill a syringe and slowly push the burn into his veins, excitedly waiting for the rush to set in so his pain would stop. He was unaware that she didn't do the same as I imagined she told him she would. The thoughts and details of that night still run rampant in my head, each scenario more sinister than the last. The hardest to accept, to heal from, is the unknown of it all. The uncertainty of what happened after he was shot up, after he decided to take a shower, after it all. That is the cold that set in and made itself a home in my soul and still lingers to this day. It has all but melted, aside from the portion reserved for the truth. That notion alone is a reason that I can't just 'get over it.'

I do believe that she is responsible for his death. There is a difference between causing a death and being responsible. I do believe that there was a plan to maybe not mortally hurt my brother, but to hurt him, nonetheless. The drug world is a dangerous game to play, both for the user and the dealer and everyone else in between. I do not hate my cousin, I am angry, and I am hurt, and before I started to heal, I could have done her harm. She doesn't deserve that. I know that now. I know that will never bring him back and it would add more casualties to this senseless act. It took me a long time to get to this point.

The police officers that night had her detained in the back of the cop car for her own protection that night. I was unaware of the threats being made to her that night. I was astonished at the implication that any harm would have been done to her, looking back now, it would have been me. When all of your sensibilities are gone, rationalization goes with it. It was me they were protecting her from. Me the hot-tempered baby sister who saw her as a murderer at that time. I never made any threats to her, I never said a word about it, but it would have been me.

So, my New Years are a little different nowadays. A constant reminder of the cold that coursed through my veins, of the detrimental state I was in. I celebrate my anniversary and the complete revolution around the sun with a humbled spirit and clearer outlook. I spent an eternity in darkness, afraid of the light. What I have taken away from all this is that life needs to be lived now. Anger, rage, grief, they all have a time and a place, but need to be acknowledged, dealt with and then released. It is never a good thing to be stuck in any context, especially being stuck in the poisonous quicksand of emotion. These emotions I was feeling, am feeling, are all normal. What wasn't normal was my obsession and addiction to them. I let the cold infiltrate my veins and take control of my senses. I once again sought out anything to take the pain away instead of dealing with it head on.

I absolutely hate the phrase, *'that which does not kill, makes you stronger,'* No it doesn't. I was not strong; I was weak, and I was broken, and it almost killed me too. Trauma is not something to be glorified but recognized. It needs to be honored in a way of yes it happened, yes it broke me, and yes, I can rise above it all. I look around with my mind's eye at the ashes of it and I scoop it up in my hands and let it fall between my fingers like sand. I welcome it to come to the surface and flood my senses so that I can rid it from my body, cleanse my soul of the tar that bogs it down. I now honor that cold and respect its power, if I don't, I am useless against its pull. I accepted the death of my brother, and I am hopeful I will be successful in my pursuit of complete and utter healing. I love the moon more every time I see it. I like to imagine that when he causes me to look up at him and all his glory, my brother lounges on its edge, smiling that million dollar smile down at me.

My brother was laid to rest on January 8, 2016, surrounded by people who loved him, needed him, missed him. I did not attend his funeral, for reasons I will defend to this day, however, it was standing room only at the service and the gravesite was even more crowded. I can only hope to have such a following in my passing. My mom did a beautiful job picking out his casket and releasing balloons in his honor. The pictures that flooded my phone that day have me teary eyed to this day. It is still so hard when memories pop up on Facebook, or when I still see the pain run across my parents' faces. I now can look without turning away or quickly scrolling passed.

December of 2020, I read his obituary for the first time since he passed, while writing this. It hits a little differently now that his son is gone too. But there was something I noticed that I hadn't before. A link to plant a tree in his name. I thought, how odd to plant a tree, something that will die as well, but at the same time I thought how magnificent. It inspired me to do something for his daughter. I did not plant a tree. I planted a way for her to always have something to look up to. I had the moon and I wanted to give her the stars. I renamed a star her daddy's name and I sent it to her that Christmas. A gift her mother told me that made her cry happy/sad tears. Well, Caddiebug me too.

I hope that wherever he is, he is happy, he is free, he is living his best afterlife. I hope he knows that his baby sister will never forget him. She will never allow anyone to tarnish his name or his life. I hope he knows how much she loves him; how much she misses him every single day. I hope his son rests high with him and that he knows as well how much he is loved and missed. I hope his daughter never forgets the love he had for her. I hope she knows he would want her to live her best life however she wanted to live. I hope his ex-wife will always remember the good and not dwell on the bad and that she will always be family.

I hope my dad knows that he looked up to him, despite it all. I hope that Jeremy knows that he didn't come to see him locked up because he couldn't bear to see him that way and that he was Mike's hero in every story he ever told; and that my little brother knows that he was excited for him to be here. I hope my mom knows that without love there cannot be hate and that despite it all she was loved by him. I still carry a lot of his secrets and I will forever hold them close to me. I did not write this to hurt anyone, I wrote this for myself, for the love of my brother and for my own healing. I hope whoever reads these words doesn't feel my pain but honors it. I never want anyone to feel what I went through. The pain I felt was amplified by anger, rage, hate, everything dark is afraid of. I hope that having the courage to write this, to put it all on paper and to allow others a glimpse into my darkness, will help me to love the light a little more. To heal more, and if that helps anyone else, well then that is a perk in this process I suppose.

Six years, five months, and thirteen days, that is how long he has been gone so far, and I am so glad I got to spend his last night with him. I am so honored to have known him, to have loved him, to have been the one to send him home. I will always be Mike's sister. I grew up hating that nameless identity, I healed loving it. I still have my moments and days when I still feel the cold and tears stain my face. Those days when I miss him the most; the graduations of my boys, the wedding of my oldest, and all the other big events I still find myself reaching for the phone to call and tell him about. I still tell him, just not by phone. I walk outside on a clear night; I find my beloved moon and I tell him. I feel him the most on cloudy nights and the moon looks like it is resting on them. The nights where I am reminded of the pact my grief made with that celestial being that guards the night and forced me to my knees in surrender. The night I started to heal and rise above it all. The nights where the moonlight filters through the clouds, casting a blue haze on the night. Those nights I smile, close my eyes and turn my face to the moon and whisper, *'you should be here.'*

JOURNAL ENTRY   31 JAN 2016
…'I felt him today, his hand on my shoulder. It is comforting to know he is ok. He needs to know I will be ok as well and not to worry. I don't like letting other people know of these things. I try to fight them, but every once and awhile one will catch me off guard. I told him to go home, that he doesn't belong here anymore, and that he is free now'…

JOURNAL ENTRY   7 FEB 2016

"Today has been amazing so far. Haven't felt anxious or angry all day. Maybe I am just numb to it all, I don't know, but to not feel the way I have been, is a blessing that I will take in any context. I had a dream of him last night and saw him as if he were in the very room with me. I am still trying to make sense of it all… '

JOURNAL ENTRY   8 FEB 2016

'I don't like feeling antsy, can't sit still/ Always looking for something to do, never finding enough to do, or finding what would satisfy this emptiness. I am surrounded by people, but yet still so isolated. Isaiah caught me crying. I hate doing that in front of them, of anyone. It is a sign of weakness. When shouldn't I be, right? I know I need to let it all go, but when is it appropriate to do so?

JOURNAL ENTRY   11 FEB 2016

'How do I not have bad days? I try so hard not to, try to not let you being gone disrupt my life. You were my protector, my friend, my BROTHER. I counted on you . and you never let me down until now. TELL ME WHAT AM I SUPPOSED TO DO NOW? You taught me to be strong and independent, to face all my demons, but I failed to help you do the same. They are gone now and for that I am jealous of you.

Blue light night

Shadows in the night, darkness is too bright.
I want to see, but I am blinded by the powers that be.
Standing in a crowded room, noise fills the air.
All that surrounds me is silence, it's deafening,
and I am scared
I cry out to deaf ears.
I try to run, but I am stuck there.
I fall to my knees and there I stay.
It is there I begin to pray.
Grace is what I feel,
Remembering when I can no longer stand,
We are forced to kneel.
Seeking comfort in the light
From the horrors of that blue light night

The pain expressed in this piece, goes without saying. If this has hurt anyone, I am truly sorry. I needed this. I needed the healing it afforded me, the growth it gifted me and the closure. I hope that you all can take something away from this and I hope that those affected that January night, are healing. This piece was difficult beyond any words I can write or say. I am better now that I have written them. As private of a person I am, I did something unimaginable in my life, and that is allowed others, you the reader a perfect stranger, and those close to me, to see this side of me no one knew I had. The words in the journal entries are mine. It is the same journal I alluded to in these pages. It is not in its entirety as it is very private, but enough for you to see through the stained color glass I encased it in.

Made in the USA
Columbia, SC
01 October 2024